Mary Gilliatt's
SHORTCUTS
TO GREAT DECORATING

SIMPLE SOLUTIONS TO
CLASSIC PROBLEMS

Mary Gilliatt's
SHORTCUTS
TO GREAT DECORATING

SIMPLE SOLUTIONS TO CLASSIC PROBLEMS

First published in 1991 by
Stoddart Publishing Co. Limited
34 Lesmill Road
Toronto, Canada
M3B 2T6

Published in Great Britain by
Conran Octopus Limited
37 Shelton Street
London, England
WC2H 9HN

Canadian Cataloguing in Publication Data
Gilliatt, Mary
Short cuts to great decorating
ISBN 0-7737-5437-7
1. Interior decoration – Amateurs' manuals.
I. Title.
NK2115.G54 1991 747 C91-093285-9

Printed and bound in Hong Kong

CONTENTS

INTRODUCTION

Great decorating is, to me, the art of making rooms feel as good as they look. It is as much about comfort and compromise and rooms that work well for their purpose, as it is about how rooms look. Most especially, it is making the best of what we have already and what we can afford to add, with style and grace and occasionally gusto.

As I see it, great decorating should not be dependent on money or splendid possessions and acquisitions, or beautifully proportioned rooms. All that is the stuff of *grand* decorating: lovely to look at, often inspiring, but very little to do with the way most of us live today.

Of course, decorating will take a special kind of confidence which initially most of us lack. It is hard to think of laying out precious funds on what might prove to be mistakes, just as it is easy to get panicked by lack of time.

Happily, there are proven antidotes to combat lack of confidence – nuggets of special decorator information; tried and tested professional methods; useful recipes for space and lighting; wall, floor and window treatments, and above all, hundreds of shortcuts that save time or money and sometimes both. I have, inevitably, learned and practised them in my years of decorating, writing about decorating and examining other people's decorating all over the world. And that is exactly what this book is about: Shortcuts to Great Decorating. Read about them. Look at them. Try them – they all work.

Mary Gilliatt

FAST FORWARD

Ingenuity and imagination can be far more productive and rewarding than a vast decorating budget at your disposal

THE STARTING BLOCKS

The key to creating pleasing interiors is to find your own sense of style, not in a haphazard way, but rather through a concentrated exercise in visual perception.

First, take a long, hard look at rooms you find appealing – in other people's homes, room settings in stores and show houses, or interiors in books, magazines, paintings, on television and in films. Take in every part of the room, from its basic structure – walls, ceiling, floor and windows – to architectural details such as fireplaces, mouldings, skirting boards (baseboards) and door surrounds. Then note the combinations of colour, lighting, texture, pattern and arrangement of furnishings.

It is worth spending time trying to analyse what appeals to you, and why – developing strong, clear ideas will help you to avoid expensive mistakes.

Subtle use of greys, white and black adds a subtle distinction to a plain kitchen.

Colour with Confidence

As you learn to look at rooms in this way, you will discover that you favour certain colour schemes over others. When it comes to decorating, many people opt for 'neutral' muted shades they think will be easier to live with. The surest way to create a uniquely stylish room – rather than merely a 'safe' one – is to be confident, trust your eye, and use the colours that have appealed to you consistently.

OPPOSITE *Stencilling is a fast way of livening up an otherwise undistinguished space.*

BELOW *Curtains frame a charming display in this internal window.*

It's a Great Idea...

- Collect snippets of fabric, samples of wallpaper and pictures of rooms from magazines that attract your attention
- Sort through your collection, analysing the different elements, such as colours and styles of furniture – you may be surprised by the similarities that occur and the decorating themes that emerge

The Style File

- How is direct and indirect lighting used in successful interiors?
- If the atmosphere seems to be soft and inviting, work out where the light sources are and how they are positioned
- Is indirect lighting used behind plants, furnishings, in corners or on top of windows?
- Does this indirect lighting come from uplights placed on the floor or from strips concealed behind pelmets or valances?
- How many reading lamps are there, and are they well positioned?
- Are objects such as paintings, plants and pieces of sculpture lit by spotlights (which give a directional beam of light) or wall-washers (which 'wash' the wall with an even stream of light)?

. . . Floors? . . . Windows?

- Is the floor a hard surface composed of wood, brick, tiles, vinyl or linoleum, softened with scattered rugs, or is it fitted with wall-to-wall carpet?
- Is the surface painted or decorated in some unusual way?
- In your favourite rooms, what part do the window treatments play in the look of the whole?
- Are they made up of blinds, curtains, drapes, swags of fabric, or a combination of various techniques?
- Are they finished with borders, trims, fringes or tie-backs and if so, how are they used?
- Is there some sort of heading such as a pelmet or valance, or are curtains simply suspended on a brass rod or gathered on to a track?

The Finishing Touches

- Are the furnishings antique, reproduction, thoroughly modern, or a mixture?
- What period or style do they evoke?
- How do they complement the rest of the room's fittings?
- How are the upholstery fabrics, shapes and textures combined?
- What rôle do the accessories play in the overall scheme? Every room acquires polish from its accessories, from the minimalist space adorned with a single flower in a plain glass vase, to the Victorian-style parlour crammed with pot plants and trinkets

STYLE SENSE

As you learn to analyse the components of a room, you are acquiring the kind of confidence that will enable you to make your own choices with some certainty.

You are also on the way to developing a sure sense of decoration – knowing exactly what you want to achieve and how to go about it. In short, you are starting to develop your own *style.*

Whether you live in a house, apartment or even one room, it is important that you feel at ease there – this means that the interior should reflect your own personality, interests and taste. Use the skills you have acquired through looking at other rooms to assess what you have got, what you can work on and what has to go. Start with the shell and carefully examine the walls, floor, windows and lighting before working out a plan of action which should include everything from structural repairs to what furniture you need.

Fast Steps to a Perfect Finish

- ► On the whole, dark- or warm-coloured walls, whether painted or papered, have a richer, more 'finished' look than plain white or pale-coloured ones
- ► Lengths of slim gilt moulding used for picture framing look wonderful on dark walls, stuck just below the ceiling, or used to form wall panels
- ► Pale colours can also be made to look more interesting with a paper border, or even a border of grosgrain or velvet ribbon stuck on to the wall with strong bonding glue
- ► If the floor is wood and in reasonable condition, it can be stripped and sanded – you could also bleach or stain it for a stronger effect – before polishing
- ► If the floor is in a poor state, it can be painted or decorated and, in either case, softened with a rug or two
- ► A shabby carpet can be disguised with rugs or sheets of primed yachting canvas rolled out and tacked down at the edges of the room
- ► For windows, buy the cheapest white paper roller blinds which can be left as they are or painted, pending more luxurious treatments
- ► For a more elegant look, drape and loop white muslin over a plain wooden pole and let it cascade down both sides of the window to the floor

Lighting – The Instant Transformer

- ► Central ceiling lights can cast a harsh, unattractive light, so try to detach them if you can. If this is not possible, fit a dimmer switch to add a degree of subtlety and make a feature of the light fitting with an interesting shade
- ► Attractive supplementary lighting can be provided with table lamps, augmented with uplights placed in corners and behind clusters of plants
- ► Uplights add an extra dimension to a room at night, casting wonderful shadows as well as light onto walls and ceiling. Good Art Deco reproductions are now widely available

Flavour of Furniture

At this stage, it is also very important to consider the kind of furniture and furnishings you have already, as well as those you hope to acquire.

Themes and motifs inspired by favourite pieces can be picked up and adapted for use on walls, floors, woodwork and window treatments. For instance, a decorative pelmet on a bookcase can be repeated in a *faux* cornice. In this way, however humble-looking your furniture, you will create a harmonious setting that can be added to later, time and budget permitting.

ABOVE Filmy curtains can be draped over an antique tester bed to make an instant canopy.

TOP An inspired but simple paint treatment draws the eye to a stunning landscape.

LEFT Painting walls and furniture shades of blue-green unifies an eclectic collection of objects.

This will also help you to achieve one of the basic tenets of successful decorating which is this: at no stage should your room look underfurnished or bare (except as part of a deliberately Minimalist look) or uninteresting and cold.

Planned to Perfection

If you are working within a limited budget, it is a good idea to work out a stage-by-stage plan. Decide what you must do now, what you would like to do in the future, and where you can reasonably compromise. Buy furnishings when you can afford them, and use pleasing and inexpensive substitutes in the interim. Do important behind-the-scenes work, such as rewiring, *before* covering the walls with expensive wallpaper, but a coat of paint is always a cheap temporary measure.

SPACE SAVERS

Get your space into good shape and the rest of your scheme should fall quickly and easily into place

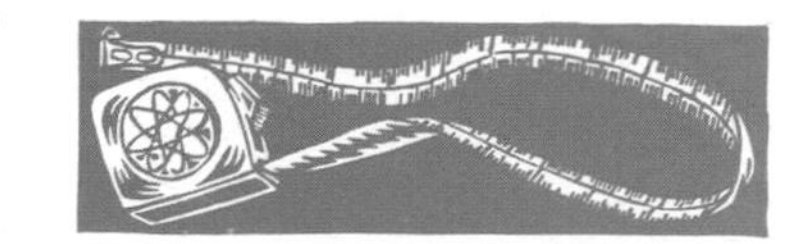

An all-white colour scheme can make any space seem larger.

TOO SMALL?

Most of us are not totally satisfied with the space in our homes. Rooms are usually too small, too dark, too low or too awkward for easy furniture arrangement.

If your rooms are small, there are two basic decorating approaches to choose from. The first defies the idea that small spaces are a disadvantage. Rich colours and textures, a few pieces of over-sized furniture and a flamboyant gesture with easy-to-apply architectural details add up to a sumptuous, memorable room that glories in the confines of its own space. The second method seeks to deny the space limitations by using pale colours, geometric tricks and expanses of mirror to expand the boundaries of the room. Here, furniture should be carefully chosen to complement the airy, spacious atmosphere created.

Expanding the Space

Most people with small rooms to decorate wish to accentuate a feeling of space rather than highlight the lack of it. This can be done in a number of ways and to such effect that it is possible for an empty, undecorated room to look less spacious than the same room after it has been decorated and filled with furniture, such is the power of paint, light and furnishings.

- Using paint with a gloss finish will reflect the light and help blur the confines of the available space even further
- Wallpapers with geometric patterns tend to create a feeling of perspective. Trellis patterns, or large, open geometric designs on a white or pale background, will add an illusion of depth
- You could also attach garden trellis to the walls. This should be painted in a contrasting colour to its background: white over blue, green with white, blue or yellow, are all good combinations
- In a small room, floor and window treatments should not be allowed to dominate. Plain carpet or painted floorboards and windows dressed with simple blinds or curtains will enhance the feeling of spaciousness
- Details should be kept simple – for example, try removing solid wooden doors altogether, or replacing them with glass-panelled ones to give a light and airy feel to any room

Reflected Glory

Of all the illusory devices used to open up small spaces, the most dramatic and versatile is mirror. Mirror panels, though not inexpensive, will make an outstanding difference to the apparent space and light in a room. Mirror tiles are much easier on the purse and, if not quite such stunning manipulators of wall space, are also very effective.

- A mirror panel placed between a pair of windows will give the illusion of a whole wall of windows, especially if the panel is the same size as the window frames
- Mirror panels cut to the size of a room's windows, then framed and hung on the opposite wall, will give the impression that there are windows on both sides of the room, as well as reflecting extra light
- A whole wall of mirror, used from floor to ceiling, will give the impression of at least double the actual space. Looped-back curtains on either side will create the illusion of an arch leading into a second room
- Floor-to-ceiling mirror either side of a chimney breast will make the fireplace look like it is the central point of a much longer room
- Putting plants against a mirror panel will exaggerate the amount of foliage by day; uplights placed behind the plants will add an extra, glamorous dimension at night. (Be careful to avoid scorching the plants with the bulbs)

ABOVE *To make the most of a narrow room, warm yellow walls are cleverly delineated by a bordered white dado rail.*

OPPOSITE *A mirrored wall 'doubles' the size of this living room, as well as heightening the impact of objects on the mantel.*

- A very small room can be made to look octagonal and far more interesting by placing slim panels of mirror obliquely across its four corners
- Replace the upper wooden or glass panels on doors with mirrored glass
- Remember: never shine light directly into a mirror – the angle of the light is crucial – otherwise you will be blinded by the glare

TOO HIGH?

The received wisdom is that a high ceiling makes for a gracious room. But, if it is too high, the space may seem uncomfortably out of proportion and intimidating.

Sometimes, structural solutions to such problems are tolerably simple to undertake with the correct professional advice. For example, a partition wall between two rooms could be knocked down, either partially or totally, thus lessening the impact of over-high ceilings and carrying with it the added bonus of increased natural light. This kind of demolition is not a time-consuming process, so the labour costs will not be high; before the work begins make sure that the wall is not load bearing. The main expense will come from patching up the floor and ceiling and creating a unified decorating scheme for your new room.

A quicker alternative would be to create the impression of a lower ceiling by emphasizing horizontal planes. This can be done very simply by, for example, fitting a densely patterned carpet or painting strong horizontal bands of colour around the room, or creating a dado or wainscoting.

Quick Remedies

If you do not want to carry out expensive structural alterations, there are plenty of relatively simple techniques you can use to your advantage. Paint, wallpaper and fabric can all be used to create the impression of better proportions in a room.

- Dark paint with a matt finish will give the ceiling the appearance of being lower than it actually is. A dark stained, painted or carpeted floor, combined with the darker ceiling, will enhance this effect considerably
- As with rooms that are too small, you could add interest with paper incorporating a geometric or trellis design. A painted mural or scenic-patterned paper would have a similar effect. In a child's room you could add a dado rail and paint beneath it with blackboard paint – an instant 'canvas'!
- One luxurious, but not necessarily expensive, way to counteract an over-high ceiling is to create a tented room by attaching fabric stapled on to battens to the wall. Any light behind the false ceiling will be filtered and diffused, creating a soft, intimate atmosphere
- One mirrored or arched wall will make the room seem longer and therefore more in proportion

Horizontal Hold

A conventional method of 'lowering' the height of a ceiling is to emphasize horizontal lines by adding dados, skirting boards (baseboards), picture rails and cornices. But why not adapt some of the classic solutions and give them a modern twist?

- A deep cornice can be further emphasized by the addition of a distinctive stencilled or paper border or frieze. Paper borders and friezes can be fixed with wallpaper paste
- Break up the wall space with a dado made by fixing lengths of moulding at waist height and either papering or painting the area below with a contrasting or darker colour to the walls above. Or you could use paint or paper to create the effect of a panelled dado
- Instead of adding mouldings, borders or friezes, make your own version with a series of decorative plates, saucers or small, framed prints hung side by side
- Eye-catching headings for windows distract the eye from the height of the ceiling. You could decorate a shaped pelmet board with fabric, paint or stencils, or for a quick but often stunning effect, simply wind swags of fabric, such as muslin or cheesecloth, around a curtain pole or rod

ABOVE Paper friezes are available in different widths and in lots of different designs. Most need to be pasted but some are self-adhesive.

TOP The soaring space of this white attic has been denied by two skilfully positioned rows of lights suspended from the ceiling beams.

OPPOSITE For tall rooms with little period distinction add a picture rail and paint the area above in a different shade to 'lower' the height of the ceiling.

POOR PROPORTIONS?

These days a perfectly proportioned room is all too rare. Too many recent buildings seem to encourage cramming in the greatest number of rooms at the expense of good proportions. This, coupled with badly done conversions of old single family houses into small apartments, has rendered the perfectly proportioned room a rare thing indeed.

Unappealing spaces of this kind range from narrow, truncated rooms to the often charming, but small-windowed, low spaces of country cottages and the tiny front and back rooms of modest nineteenth- and early-twentieth-century urban houses. Fortunately, there are innumerable ways of disguising and enhancing such awkwardly shaped rooms.

ABOVE The mirrored wall in this small entrance hall not only gives a feeling of spaciousness but increases the amount of light. Note the unobtrusive slide-in cupboard.

LEFT Beading has been added to the wainscoting and the cupboard for a stylish finish in this cosy bathroom.

RIGHT This living room garners distinction from its white-on-white scheme, a delicately bordered ceiling and the contrast of dark furniture and framed pictures.

Crafty Camouflage

Paint and wallpaper are effective disguises for many architectural sins.

- One paint colour covering ceiling, walls and woodwork will camouflage many of the irritating idiosyncracies of a badly proportioned room. Rooms that get a lot of natural light could benefit by being painted in white or a pale colour; dark rooms usually look better painted a rich, warm colour, and *faux* finishes can transform a hitherto unappealing space
- Vertical stripes will make rooms seem a good deal taller
- Geometric patterns can give the illusion of more space
- A different wallpaper above the dado will add graciousness to any room
- Carefully chosen florals can make dull spaces infinitely more appealing
- *Faux* finish wallpapers draw attention away from the surface imperfections. A finishing coat of eggshell polyurethane will give an enviably professional result, but first ensure the colours do not run by testing a piece of the wallpaper

The Great Cover-Up

A soft, sumptuous look can be achieved with inexpensive cheesecloth or cotton hung from rods all around the room like curtains and drawn back over doors and windows. Alternatively, you could create a more strongly architectural impression by lining the walls with bookcases. Continue them around windows and doors so that both appear to be recessed and, if the room is rather small, leave further recesses for sofas and desks so that they appear to tuck snugly into the shelves. Both of these techniques disguise the meanest proportions in a stylish way.

It's a Great Idea...

- Use accent lighting to draw attention to a beautiful object or painting and away from irregularly shaped walls
- A rug with a bold horizontal design will make an enormous difference to a narrow space – a *trompe l'oeil* version would be just as good for the job

DOUBLING UP

An effective way to treat limited space is to create dual-purpose rooms. With clever planning and ingenuity, all the space in a small apartment or house can be utilized in the fullest way possible.

Living rooms can comfortably take in both work and dining areas. Dining rooms can double as studies, playrooms and occasional guest rooms. Kitchens can certainly be combined with dining rooms, as well as home offices if you can install a separate working surface. With the help of a screen or substantial piece of furniture, spacious halls and landings can include dining space, work areas and space for guests. Bedrooms can easily be combined with work rooms and libraries. Moderately sized bathrooms make excellent exercise spaces.

Dual-Purpose Strategy

Once you decide to make a room dual purpose or 'multi-functional', it becomes a question of ingenuity.

- A good way to add a work space into a studio apartment is to create a platform bed, with shelves and desk underneath
- A living room can be transformed from a day-time playroom into an elegant space to receive dinner guests by sweeping all the toys either under a large, skirted table, or into a chest of drawers kept specifically for that purpose
- It is possible to divide up a long, narrow room by installing three shallow platforms, each one allocated a different purpose such as dining/work space, sitting/spare bed space and regular sleeping space
- In similar single-room dwellings, the Murphy bed (a bed that folds up into a wall for storage) is supremely practical
- Another stylish way to combine sleeping and living space would be to place a large double bed in the centre of a room – during the day this can be made to look like back-to-back sofas by the simple expedient of putting a large back rest in the middle and then heaping it with cushions on either side. A futon is also useful as it can be rolled up and stored during the day or used as seating

Hidden Extras

Clearly, if you want to put up overnight guests on a sofa-bed in the living room, study, or even the hall or landing, it would be helpful if you could also provide some inconspicuous clothes storage.

An attractive brass hook or two on the back of the door helps, as does a sturdy screen with pegs screwed into the back of the frame. A chest of drawers (with at least one empty drawer) in close proximity is also useful. Another ingenious way of providing extra clothes storage is by making hanging space behind stationary curtains on a window wall. The concealing curtains remain closed, covering the wall and clothes, while the curtains over the actual window can be drawn back and forth.

Extra seating, too, can be provided in a number of inconspicuous ways, ranging from window seats, club fenders around fires, attractive folding chairs (stored on sturdy wall hooks) to large floor cushions.

ABOVE LEFT Japanese-style sliding screens separate a sleeping platform from the living area.

LEFT A bed built into an alcove makes the best use of the space available and gives this room a double role without sacrificing style.

OPPOSITE Elegant blue-and-white fabric covers a dining area squeezed into a tiny hallway.

Instant Solution:
CURTAINED OFF

Thick, full curtains falling to the floor may be caught back with tasselled cords to open up the space by day, and drawn tight at night on more formal occasions – then the dining table can be covered in a long starched linen cloth, and the room lit by the flickering light of candles, which dramatize the strong architectural leaves of the large potted plant. It is a versatile room. Polished wooden floors are softened with rugs, the wrought-iron chairs are eccentric enough to pass as casual garden furniture or elegantly sculptural, and ornamentation is kept to a minimum. Everything in the room is the product of a fertile imagination rather than a large budget. ABOVE

Instant Solution:
SHELVE IT

In studio apartments, every inch of space should be used to fullest advantage. Here, spatial diversity is created by an easy-to-construct floor-to-ceiling slatted and shelved screen which separates a cosy sitting area from the dining table and study space without blocking out natural light. An open-plan kitchen (unseen) fills the corner of the room. A sense of luxury and richness is created by contrasting textures: russet upholstery fabric on the chairs; the slick chrome of the uplight; wood veneer on the side table and the soft quality of the rugs. Over half of the wall space is covered in practical built-in bookshelves crammed with colourful books and interesting objects, adding to the overall interest of the room. RIGHT

Instant Solution: DIFFERENT LEVELS

Platforms are one of the quickest ways of rationalizing a small amount of space – they can be simply made from sets of drawers, doors or planks of wood. Here, the upper level acts as a desk top as well as a bed base. ABOVE

Instant Solution: HIDDEN ASSETS

A double bed neatly slides out of the useful storage space underneath a low platform in this well-planned studio apartment. Other space-expanders are the pale colours of the walls and furnishings, glass shelves and table and a window-like mirror behind shelves of plants. TOP

ARCHITECTURAL INTEREST

Adding period details to walls, ceiling and doors can turn an undistinguished room into somewhere really special

Transform a fire hole with a grand mantel and unusual ornaments.

FIREPLACES

Few things provide as appealing a focal point as a beautiful fireplace with flames flickering in the grate. There are many ways to improve the appearance of a fireplace, or you may have a cosmetic solution, creating an interesting focal point without lighting a fire. It's amazing what can be done, for example, with an arrangement of dried flowers.

Despite their importance to the room, many old fireplaces are curiously misproportioned and ugly, with ungainly tiles and hearths. You may even have the frustrating problem of having a fireplace that does not work because its flues have been blocked deliberately, or one that is purely ornamental with no chimney behind it.

New Looks for Old

If you are considering replacing a fireplace because you find it aesthetically unappealing, examine it carefully. Tap surfaces to ascertain whether they are stone or wood, and always look behind boarding. Beautifully grained wood, handsome marble and attractive, unusual tiles have all been found under the most unpromising of surface treatments, painted or boarded over by a previous owner.

- If the wood is good enough, strip and polish it
- Poor quality wood looks better painted either plain white or given a *faux* marble or *faux bois* finish
- Ugly tiling is costly to remove, but you could simply board it over or place new tiles over the top
- The boarding can be *faux* marbled so that it looks like the genuine thing, or it can be tiled with mirror to add extra light and sparkle to your room
- For a quick face-lift you can always paint tiles – give them a coat of metal primer before painting them in your chosen gloss or semi-gloss colour
- An effective form of tile camouflage often used by decorators is to use tile design contact paper. If done carefully, this quick and inexpensive method can produce very effective results. After sticking the paper to the original tiles, you could use artists' oil colours to age the surface and then apply a coat of polyurethane varnish

It's a Great Idea...

A fireplace can make a stylish contribution to your room scheme.

- You could always remove the mantel altogether, simply leaving a framed hole in which to burn logs
- Simply add a stunning mantel without the side supports surrounding the fire-hole. Antique mantels look wonderful treated in this way
- Marble, brass or steel brackets placed at mantel height above the fire-hole with a sheet of toughened glass or stainless steel bolted across the top create a distinctive mantel shelf and a worthy centrepiece
- Wooden or glass shelves fitted into a redundant fireplace recess provide an attractive way to display plants, books and pretty objects
- A bulky stereo can be fitted quite neatly into the space previously occupied by an old grate
- Board over a disused fire-hole and create a *trompe l'oeil* fireplace
- In a child's room, an architectural fireplace could be turned into an ingenious dolls' house

RIGHT *The severe lines of this fireplace are softened by white paint, making it a good background for an interesting collection of objects.*

OPPOSITE *Classical columns outline this fireplace, the focal point of a comfortable living room. In the summer months, a low stool fits neatly into the space.*

Something for Nothing

If your fireplace works but seems cosmetically irredeemable, it is worth replacing it with something the same size. Before you launch into a potentially expensive fireplace-hunt, look in skips or dumpsters outside old house renovations, and make regular rounds of junk yards and demolition merchants. You never know what you might find.

Do remember to keep a note of the height and depth of the fireplace opening on you at all times – you never know when you might find a suitable candidate. If your search proves fruitless, however, renovated and reproduction fireplaces are widely available but at a price.

WINDOWS

If you are lucky enough to have graceful windows or particularly interesting views, there are many ways of drawing attention to them.

You could paint the frames in a contrasting colour to the walls and use plain blinds rather than heavy curtains or drapes. If you have shutters, pick out the panels in paint, exaggerate them with stencilled decoration, or make a dramatic statement with Mondrianesque blocks of colour.

To emphasize wonderful views, treat the window like a picture frame with a simple blind that can be drawn for privacy or in bad weather, without the distraction of elaborate window treatments.

Simple Window Dressing

Less handsome windows, or those with poor views, can be improved in a variety of ways.

- They can be stripped back to the original wood. This can then be sealed or stained with a coloured or wood stain, depending on the rest of your room scheme
- Wooden windows will look more substantial with the addition of fine mouldings such as beading to the glazing bars
- A very distinctive look can be achieved, particularly in tall rooms, by adding arched or rounded architraves, available from specialist shops, or you could paint them on yourself
- If privacy is important, louvred shutters give immediate distinction and crisp lines to your windows
- Half shutters are also a good idea, providing privacy without losing light
- Flat sheets of muslin suspended from thin rods show off surrounding frames

A Touch of Tracery

Give a Gothic or Arabian accent to your room by painting elaborate tracery around your window frames and even on the glass itself. Buy paint specially formulated for use on glass from a good artists' supply store and use pre-cut or home-made stencils to get a crisp line.

ABOVE LEFT The blue of the squares and diamonds inset into plain leaded windows has been picked up in the tiled splashback, the tablecloth and other kitchen accessories.

LEFT Filling an alcove window with plants, and adding a padded window seat and elegant curtains creates a charming corner in this stylish cottage.

FAR LEFT A boxed seat with a panelled front is a simple way of dealing with deeply recessed windows. The panel is lined up with the dado rail and is flush with the wall.

OPPOSITE Gothic-style windows dominate, their shape echoed in the radiator cover. The beautiful rose quilt has a stylized medieval-type pattern, in keeping with the Gothic theme.

MAGIC MOULDINGS

Attractive architectural details provide variety and add interest to a room. If your home lacks them, it is possible to add good details yourself.

More and more companies are now producing a wide choice of good reproduction classical mouldings in fibreglass and polystyrene (which are very light and simple to apply), as well as in the more traditional materials of plaster and wood. Alternatively, visual interest can be added just as effectively using decorative wallpaper borders or paper copies of classical mouldings – a less expensive option for instant effect.

It's a Great Idea...

- To make a modern statement in an architecturally featureless room, paint bands of colour on the wall where the skirting board, dado and picture rail would be
- Add an extra layer of moulding to the door surround, or consider fitting an architrave if you have high enough ceilings to take one
- Experiment with stencilled or free-hand painting to create *faux* architectural detailing, such as cornices and dado rails

Mouldings in No Time

- If you do not want to run to the expense of buying 'proper' reproductions, you can attach lengths of ordinary bolection moulding to the wall. These can then be painted or stained in a contrasting colour to emphasize the different areas of walls and ceiling. Further decoration can be added with a paper or stencilled border placed just below the new mouldings
- One way of creating inexpensive but luxurious-looking mouldings is to use lengths of carved picture framing, either gilded or stained, or even 'mahoganized'
- Thin gilt strips look especially good when used to finish fabric-covered walls. If you buy undecorated lengths of picture frame, you can paint or gild them to match your scheme
- Similar lengths of bolection moulding or picture frame can be used to create effective dados and panelling
- Narrow skirting boards (baseboards) look much more substantial if an extra layer of moulding is added along the top. For example, a detailed piece of edging added to the kind of plain skirting found in many twentieth-century houses will create a more sophisticated finish
- Wooden mouldings, straight or curved, are available ready-made for flush doors, cupboard fronts and kitchen units

New Ideas for Old

In older houses, skirting boards can look very good stripped to their original wood, or stained if the wood is in bad condition. Combed or dragged mouldings were popular in the nineteenth century.

BELOW Apply wide moulding to make a rectangular, panelled effect on a plain wall.

OPPOSITE For a subtle effect, downplay applied mouldings by clever dragging and marbling.

Instant Solution:
A GLASS SHELF

Mantelpieces can be very expensive to install. A clever solution is created in this modern room by bolting a cut-to-order length of thick, bevelled glass on to a pair of marble brackets. ABOVE

Instant Solution:
FRAME IT

To transform a simple, doored sink unit add readily available side panels carved to look like pillars. RIGHT

Instant Solution:
ADD DECORATIVE DETAILS

A painted overmantel adds special character to this room. FAR RIGHT

Instant Solution:
UNIFY WITH COLOUR

Painting the door surround and fireplace in the same shade of blue-green as the upper walls of the adjoining room not only unites the two spaces but defines the different areas, and complements the antique pieces of furniture. ABOVE

Instant Solution:
THE FINISHING TOUCH

Adding a delicate paper border beneath the cornice and trompe l'oeil *ropes and tassels around prints gives this pretty bedroom a classical air. Matching the edging on the hanging cabinet to the red borders around the pictures and using fine piping on the soft furnishings further emphasize the really stylish effect yet warm, intimate feel of the room.* TOP

STORAGE SOLUTIONS

Storage space lurks in almost all homes – it's just a simple matter of finding it and then making the most of it

ON THE MOVE

To the wistful adage that you cannot be too rich or too thin could be added 'or have enough storage'. For however sparse your possessions seem to be when you first set up home, they grow at an alarming rate.

For your own peace of mind, it is vital that you devise a convenient storage system, however limited the space at your disposal may be.

First, work out what kind of storage would work best in each area – living rooms, dining rooms, halls, bedrooms and kitchens all have very different storage requirements and it is sensible to plan in advance rather than face the frustrating problem of inappropriate or inadequate storage later. Decide what should be out of sight and what can be left on display; what storage can be built in and what should be movable.This is particularly important if you live in rented accommodation or if your think your lifestyle is going to change drastically in the next few years (perhaps by the addition of children) – it is in these kinds of situations that free-standing storage comes into its own.

Simple Options

There are many reasons for having free-standing, as opposed to fitted or built-in, storage, ranging from the aesthetic and the financial to living in rented accommodation where building in storage may be neither permissible nor desirable. What you must remember is that free-standing storage has to be reasonably attractive in its own right, as well as useful, otherwise it will simply look untidy.

- It may be inappropriate to build closets and cupboards in a beautifully proportioned, well detailed room. Instead, look out for handsome old bookcases, *armoires* and chests
- In a large living and dining area, free-standing shelf or storage units can also act as room dividers
- Functional storage for bedrooms is frequently expensive. But with a little imagination it is quite possible to find cheap, good-looking solutions, such as stacking wire or plastic baskets, or even filing cabinets, to keep your underwear, shirts and sweaters
- Another effective and versatile piece of storage furniture is the standard metal gym locker which can be picked up very cheaply and painted either in a bright colour or to blend in with the walls
- If the high-tech appearance of this kind of furniture is out of keeping with the rest of your room, you can conceal it behind a screen – for good measure, add hooks for clothes to the back of the sturdy screen, too

LEFT A pair of filing cabinets is transformed by a series of still-lifes.

OPPOSITE BELOW Dressers invariably make handsome as well as capacious storage pieces.

OPPOSITE ABOVE An armoire *provides storage, and the chest is used for changing the baby.*

It's a Great Idea...

Many small, inexpensive items can be used to create flexible storage for small objects. Here are some you might like to try:

- Wicker baskets for clothes, linen, books and papers
- Printers' type trays for small items such as sewing or office equipment
- Orange boxes or wine crates for effective impromptu shelves
- Second-hand stainless steel office or hospital trolleys for bathroom or kitchen equipment
- Glass jars for reels of cotton, embroidery silks, odd balls of wool – anything brightly coloured

BUILT-IN SOLUTIONS

Before building in storage, take a long, hard look at the room or rooms in which you want to construct it, noting the proportions, architectural elements, details, recesses and any obviously usable walls or corners.

The ideal is to extend cupboards or closets to ceiling height, or finish them with an appropriate moulding, cornice or pediment. Any moulding that will be concealed should be matched, and continued along the fronts of the new storage. This attention to detail makes all the difference.

Behind Closed Doors

- Cupboards or closets can be made to look as if they are a continuation of the wall, or panelled like existing doors to the room and can then be either painted or covered with wallpaper or fabric
- In a smallish room, incorporate large objects of furniture, like a sofa, within a wall of storage – creating an alcove will make the room *seem* bigger and neater. Cupboards or shelves can be continued across the top of the alcove
- In a bedroom, dressing table, drawers, shelves, as well as hanging space can all be incorporated into wall storage, which can be continued around windows and above doors
- When planning storage walls that are to include deep objects such as televisions and stereos bear in mind that the deepest piece of equipment should determine the overall depth
- If this is too space-consuming, build deep cupboards or closets underneath with narrower shelves above, forming a stylish break-front cabinet
- If you are investing in a ready-made storage wall, check that your appliances will fit neatly inside recesses
- In older homes, hardwood mouldings can be glued to cupboard doors and shelf edges before painting to give furniture a style in keeping with other structural details of the room

Under and Away

Extra storage can be provided by adding lift-up lids and under-seat bins to window seats, or a row of built-in seating fitted along one wall or across the corner of a room.

ABOVE An easily constructed partition creates invaluable walk-in storage.

TOP Beautiful pull-out baskets fit snugly into shelves edged with a patterned border.

OPPOSITE To maximize limited storage space build shelves that reach to the ceiling and frame the door. An ornate antique cabinet with its drawers decorated with Indian dancers, musicians, and flowers, is an unusual contrast.

Instant Solution: COVER UP

A good-looking, efficient kitchen can be created quickly for a very small amount of money. Once the oven, sink and countertop were in place here, the cupboard area underneath was simply curtained over with pretty yellow-and-white PVC to match the table cover; later, cabinets could be built in. A thick wooden shelf provides extra storage space for pots and pans above the work surfaces. OPPOSITE ABOVE LEFT

Instant Solution: RECYCLING

A little imagination goes a long way when planning storage. Recycling industrial packaging is often a good approach. Here, handsome cylinders that contained rolls of fabric were turned into charming storage boxes for a number of disparate items and kept on shelves in a small hallway. The same cylinders upended make good umbrella stands. Hat boxes and plastic crates are other options. OPPOSITE BELOW LEFT

Instant Solution: FIT IT IN

In today's small apartments, many of which are squeezed into the smallest possible spaces, often no provision is made for storage. But some of the best solutions of all – and the quickest – are the easiest and most obvious. In this well-planned bedroom, a partition hides a generous closet and doubles as a sturdy headboard. Running the width of the room, a deep shelf is stacked with laundry baskets. The space underneath the bed should not be overlooked: here, you can store bulky items such as books and magazines by raising the bed higher than normal to about waist height – on a platform the amount of space available is almost doubled. In addition, doors have been replaced by curtains, thus avoiding 'lost' space behind them. In the modern living room, comfortable, cushioned seating hides clever additional storage underneath. LEFT

Instant Solution: BATHING BEAUTY

The round wicker baskets hanging from pegs on a stained wooden rack provide both practical and decorative storage. The handsome tongue-and-groove panelling used for the front of the bath and airing cupboard wedged into an alcove has been coloured a silvery grey. Note the roped beading along the edge of the bath and the fine stencilling above the basket rack. ABOVE

Instant Solution: SPRAY IT

Spray paint wicker laundry baskets to co-ordinate with the decor of the room – it is quick and easy to do. Baskets like these lilac ones provide good storage for linens and heavy winter clothing. As well, they double as a practical bedside table. OPPOSITE BELOW RIGHT

OUT OF SIGHT

Only the best planned living spaces have enough storage space. You need to work out exactly what should be stored where, and try to estimate future needs.

Clothes, linens, books, cassettes, cooking and sporting equipment, tools, toys, papers and records are the most obvious candidates for storing. All these items need their own place – in the most appropriate and logical position in the home.

There are always going to be objects which are never put away after use, often because the space allotted to them is too far away from where they are used. When you tire of tripping over children's toys in the living room and winter boots in the hall, it is time to start thinking creatively about how to store the huge quantities of impedimenta we all seem to acquire.

Squeezing in Storage

If you look around your home – however small it may be – there are bound to be places with untapped storage potential.

- One of the most popular sites for out-of-sight, out-of-mind storage is underneath beds. Obviously, the higher the base of the bed from the floor, the better the storage space for suitcases, boxes and laundry baskets
- The back of doors and shutters have great storage potential. Small objects can be displayed or concealed effectively on wire racks, narrow wooden shelves or neat hooks
- Screens are one of the most obvious concealers of necessary objects such as exercise and sports equipment, filing cabinets and papers, not to mention clothes racks, plastic storage containers, and general household accoutrements
- In busy households where living and dining rooms frequently double as

It's a Great Idea...

Take some tips from professional wardrobe organizers when it comes to sorting out your clothes, shoes and accessories.

- ► Invest in commercial clothes rails on casters to provide extra hanging space – they're cheap and invaluable
- ► Adding another rail to one side of your wardrobe approximately 75cm (2ft 6in) below the original one will allow you to hang twice the amount of shirts, blouses and jackets
- ► Wooden shoe stands on casters mean that you can simply wheel your shoes out when you want to choose a pair
- ► Wire baskets have the advantage of keeping small things tidy *and* visible
- ► Scarves and necklaces can be hung from hooks on the inside of the wardrobe door
- ► A simple coatstand in the corner of a bedroom helps enormously in relieving the load of a bulging wardrobe and helps keep the room tidy

LEFT *Disguise bulky storage boxes or unattractive trunks under handsome, brightly patterned rugs.*

OPPOSITE *Large chests like this one look beautiful and can store a surprising amount of unsightly jumble.*

BELOW *A trunk-cum-coffee table and a painted screen create hiding places for household ephemera.*

playrooms or home offices, skirted tables often prove to be an invaluable style-saver. They are extremely practical hiding places for toys, baskets, files and other more useful than decorative items although they should not be so crammed that it is impossible to put your feet under the table when sitting

- ► Old-fashioned blanket boxes are usefully dual-purpose. They are invariably deep enough to store cumbersome items, from blankets and winter clothing, to magazines, games and luggage, and they double as seating
- ► A wall of bookshelves can be made doubly useful – and child-proof – if you install deep cupboards up to around waist height
- ► The area above a door is often overlooked as storage space. Fit a simple wooden shelf and use it to display books or ornaments which can't be stored elsewhere. Blankets and linen could also be stored here

LIGHT TRANSFORMERS

A creative and well thought-out lighting scheme is the essential key to successful decorating anywhere in the home

ALL SORTS OF LIGHTING

Good lighting is essential to the sophisticated interior, although often, it is not until walls are finished and curtain treatments are firmly in place that any thought is given to the stunning effect a couple of wired-in wall lights would have on the scheme.

For those accustomed to a bright central light supplemented by the occasional floor and table lamp, the easiest way to understand all the possibilities inherent in artificial light is to think of daylight and all its subtleties – the clear, golden light of a sunny morning; the mellow, deeper light and shade of a late summer's day; the soft filtered light of early evening; the white light of snow. With some imagination and ingenuity, there is no reason at all why you should not be able to replicate an equally broad lighting spectrum in your own home with the greatest of ease.

Think Creatively!

- If you need inspiration when planning a lighting scheme, study how lights are used in a theatre
- Note the way in which the atmosphere on the set can be changed – cheered, heightened or made gloomy – simply by a slight change in the lighting
- Look at the way painters such as Caravaggio used *chiaroscuro* (contrasting light and dark) to such a strikingly dramatic effect
- If you are keener on the culinary arts, think of accent light in terms of how adding a herb or spice can make all the difference to a dish

Anything is Possible

There are three main types of lighting. In the most successful schemes, all of these three types are usually included, in various combinations.

- Ambient, background or general lighting includes the light provided by overhead fittings or spotlights, halogen floor lamps, fluorescent fixtures behind valances, wall lights and occasional table lamps. With this kind of lighting, the aim is to cast a low level of light throughout the room
- Task, or work, light includes the kind of light originating from table, desk, or adjustable floor lamps, and from fluorescent or incandescent tubes behind baffles, or spotlights above work surfaces in kitchens and laundry rooms. It should cast sufficient light on all work areas as well as creating interesting pools of light elsewhere in the room
- Accent, or decorative, lighting is used to draw attention to possessions or arrangements, as well as to add a necessary touch of drama. It includes the type of light cast by spotlights, wall washers, uplights, downlights, picture lights, table lamps, strings of tiny bulbs, oil lamps, candle- and firelight. Lights controlled by a dimmer, and turned low also fall into this category

Wall-hung swing-arm lamps don't have to be wired in under plaster.

When It Comes to Buying . . .

It can be very difficult to buy lights when you are guided, correctly, by the premise that the effect lights achieve is equally important as what the actual fittings look like. And in a crowded showroom, which is necessarily overlit, it is quite impossible to see the sort and quality of light given off by individual fittings and fixtures.

- It is, therefore, extremely important to have a good idea of the sort of light that certain bulbs and fittings cast before you enter the store
- Make a careful plan of your room, plotting existing lights and taking into account the quality of light required and the type of fitting that will suit the style of the room
- Try to ascertain what degree of manoeuvrability and subtlety you can reasonably expect from the different types of light fittings
- Consider where and in what situations they are likely to work best. (You can do this, once again, by studying each attractive lighting arrangement you come across and noting how it is achieved)
- Check whether the lighting store will allow you to take fittings home to see how they complement the room and its furnishings

RIGHT Focus on dramatic objects – such as this mature cactus – with Christmas lights.

BELOW This room provides a good example of a successfully integrated lighting scheme.

DAYLIGHT BOOSTERS

Daylight may have fascinating variety, but it does not have especially good penetrative qualities.

This means that a surprising number of rooms need some sort of artificial boost, even during the day. Rooms in buildings with narrow frontages, or in buildings closely backing up to others, will need artificial light most of the time, and if you want to take advantage of natural light for visual tasks like writing, reading, drawing, sewing and so on, you will have to sit right next to a window.

Simple and Stylish

Many people suffer from an old-fashioned aversion to turning on the lights during the day. But if you need a desk or reading light to work or read by or simply some additional lighting to cheer up a gloomy room, you should forget such prejudices.

Thankfully, it is perfectly possible to add general booster light to a room during the day without making it, literally, glaringly obvious. And, although fluorescent bulbs cast a light that is too harsh for most evening situations, they can be used effectively to simulate daylight.

- ► Simply use subtle, indirect lighting, taking great care to conceal any bulbs
- ► Useful uplights concealed behind plants and furniture, placed inside urns, or in corners will splash walls and ceilings with light without revealing the source
- ► Halogen floor lamps will give a great punch of light without being obtrusive
- ► Elliptically shaped plaster or fibreglass wall lights also create good, sophisticated background lighting

In Place of the Sun

- ► Cool white (as opposed to warm white) fluorescent tubes concealed behind pelmets or valances set above windows or behind baffles at the side of the window can give the illusion of sunlight yet, because they are concealed, the strong light is diffused. These lights should be turned on only during the day as at night the effect is incongruous
- ► Fluorescent tubes behind pelmets or valances, or placed out of sight just above cornices or mouldings also give a good indirect light

It's a Great Idea...

- ► If you have a particularly gloomy room, consider knocking a doorway or window through into an adjoining room which enjoys better natural light (for non-load-bearing walls only)
- ► Mirror panels or a mirrored screen placed alongside a 'dark' window will boost what natural light there is

LEFT Uplights placed on the floor and a bedside lamp provide daytime booster light in this Mediterranean bed alcove.

BELOW Internal openings can be used to allow natural light into internal rooms.

NEW LOOKS FOR OLD

Few of us want to rewire a home entirely, or have the opportunity to design a complicated lighting plan from scratch – generally, we have to make the most of what we have.

Luckily, the plethora of adaptors, multiple outlet or socket strips, lengths of track, portable spots, uplights, and even powerful battery-operated lamps, not to mention candle-holders, allows us to produce dramatic, and certainly very workable, lighting schemes from plug-ins and single points.

Light Shows

- Uplights make an enormous difference to the light and shade of a room. They can simply be plugged in wherever you think they will look best, to cast gentle pools of light upon walls and ceilings as well as making their own, often architectural statement
- If you have a collection of paintings and prints you want to display to their best advantage, but only have a single centre ceiling outlet, get a neat length of track which can be placed over and powered by that same single outlet; from this you can suspend a series of tiny decorative halogen spotlights
- You can also hang wallwashers from this kind of track system and bathe the whole wall with light
- A single painting over a fireplace can be illuminated by a portable spot fixture clipped to the edge of the mantelpiece and angled to its best advantage
- For a large painting or sculpture which takes up a good deal of the wall, or is in a dominant position, a spotlight could be positioned on the floor below it to provide satisfactory illumination
- Adjustable floor lights can be tipped to shine on anything you would like to illuminate in the room
- Table lamps do not have to be restricted to task lighting; they can be effective accent lighting placed in corners, under paintings or a wall of prints

Simple but Effective

- Do not forget the dramatic potential of candlelight and oil lamps. Placed on windowsills, in wall sconces and on side tables, they create a lovely mellow, welcoming light. Groups of candles of different heights look particularly good.

Safety First

Although it is possible to make stunning lighting schemes using adaptors and plug-in lights, you should always be extremely careful not to overload the circuit.

Make sure that all flexes, switches and plugs are in good order and, if you are in any doubt, get a qualified electrician to inspect your wiring.

TOP Old-fashioned gas lamps can be converted to electricity.

RIGHT Wallwashers highlight the beauty of a Biedermeier cabinet and bust.

OPPOSITE This lampshade is made from a square of fireproof fabric stretched over a frame.

SPECTACULAR EFFECTS

Once you feel more confident about the different types of lighting and become aware of its many possibilities, you can start manipulating it to create a variety of special effects.

A great help is, of course, the dimmer switch – one of the most important developments in lighting technology, it is simple to fit and can alter the mood of a room in seconds. You may wish to use light as part of a dramatic scheme or just to create a festive atmosphere for a special party. You do not need to invest in expensive, specialist equipment – most schemes can be achieved by using your imagination to adapt readily available lighting appliances (but if you are unsure about any safety aspects, check with the store or an electrician).

Tricks of Light

- ► To make rooms seem larger, flood the walls with light from bright wallwashers that are either recessed into the ceiling (if you have plaster or wood ceilings, and have enough space in between floors to accommodate the housings) or fitted to tracks 60cm (2ft) out from the walls
- ► Rooms will seem more intimate if you illuminate the space with gentle pools of light from table lamps, uplights, downlights and well-placed spots, all controlled by dimmer switches wired, if possible, to a plate at the door

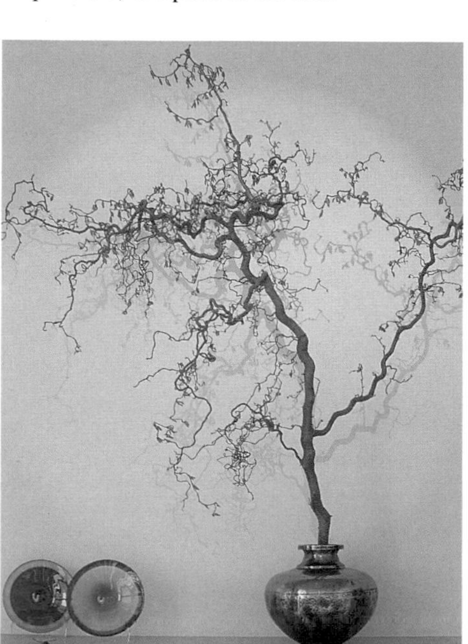

- ► You could also fix fluorescent tubes or minitracks of tiny bulbs behind small baffles set just above skirting boards, painting the baffle to blend with the rest of the moulding

Quick and Colourful

- ► You can alter the whole tone of a room simply by placing coloured bulbs in all the lamps: for a warm atmosphere, use pink bulbs in table lamps, and to make a room feel cooler use blue or green bulbs
- ► Alternatively, coloured filters or gels (from photographic stores) come in a variety of colours and can be slipped over the top of bulbs to change the mood of a room in an instant

It's a Great Idea...

Strings of Christmas tree lights do not have to be kept for the festive season:

- ► Thread them over a large plant or over bare winter branches
- ► If you have an attractive collection of books, prints or other objects, you could set the tiny lights into chiselled grooves in the front of shelves
- ► String them around doors, arches and windows to look festive

LEFT Wash dramatic arrangements with light using carefully placed spots.

RIGHT Dried flowers shield 'raw' light. Make sure you are not creating a fire hazard with this technique.

FARM

Instant Solution:
PLUG-IN UPLIGHTS

A pair of sleek architectural uplights provides subtle general lighting and emphasizes the linear style of decoration in this modern living room. They demonstrate that, in this case, less certainly is more. RIGHT

Instant Solution:
LAMP BRACKETS

The beauty of these unusual lamp brackets is that they are not wired in under the plaster. BELOW

Instant Solution:
TRADITIONAL BRASS

Flexible brass lamps are used for ambient and task lighting in this coolly decorated room. The light flexes have been cleverly threaded under the rug and up the sides of the table for near total concealment. Lamps such as these, which are usually found only on desks, are too handsome to be left in the office or study. Using them in pairs underlines their streamlined good looks.
OPPOSITE ABOVE

Instant Solution:
CAMOUFLAGE

A piece of draped fabric hanging on the wall camouflages an unusual plug-in light. It casts a soft glow on this otherwise hard-edged room, and creates textural variety on the plain white wall. To make a lamp like this one, thread thin silver florists' wire through the hems of a fireproofed fabric square. Fold the cloth over a small plug-in lamp – choose one with a longish conical shade for safety, and use a low wattage bulb – and hang on the wall. OPPOSITE BELOW

FLAWED FLOORING?

Replacing or revitalizing an existing floor may be all that's really necessary to change dramatically the way a room looks

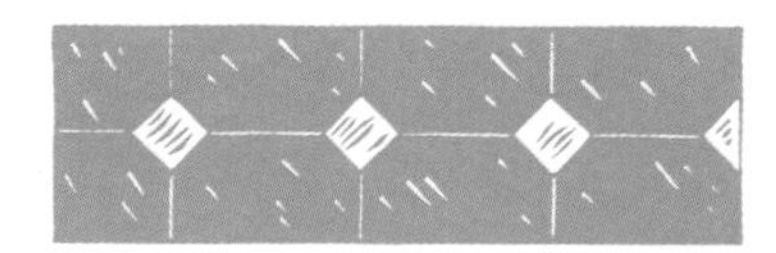

HARD-FLOOR SOLUTIONS

Flooring should be as good-looking as possible – for it is this which will anchor a room and hold its decorative scheme together. The very fact that the floor plays such a dominant role in the overall appearance makes the idea of laying a new one rather daunting, even if expense is not an issue.

Happily, except in the case of a major renovation, there is no reason to feel unduly intimidated. If floors are hard, that is to say of brick, ceramic tile, stone or marble, they should be tough enough to have sustained many years of wear and still be in good condition. Whether they are of an appealing colour and design is a different matter.

Elderly marble, dreary concrete and scruffy tiles can normally be revived, titivated or disguised using a variety of techniques – from painting, marbling, stencilling and lacquering to disguising with rugs and mats. Any of these methods can be achieved with considerably less expense, and certainly a good deal more gratification, than starting all over again.

BELOW Flagstones are coated in polyurethane varnish to make a splendid kitchen floor.

RIGHT Broken stones are much cheaper, but can be equally attractive.

Creativity at your Feet

The most obvious solution to dealing with a badly marked, stained or otherwise unattractive floor is to cover it up.

Sisal or coir matting is one of the most inexpensive floor coverings you can buy and it provides an attractive, neutral base for almost any style of furniture and decoration. Another instant solution is to cover existing carpet with stretched and painted artists' canvas.

If, however, you prefer the appearance of a hard surface, there are several methods of cosmetic revival you might like to try. The most obvious solution is to paint the floor – any paint effect you can use on walls can be adapted for this.

The key when painting a floor is to prepare the surface carefully first, ensuring that it is smooth, dust- and grease-free and clean. Be prepared to seal the paint with polyurethane annually, however, as unsealed paint does tend to wear off hard surfaces quite quickly. One of the advantages of sealing is that it then does not matter what type of paint you use to make your design.

Polishing it Off

A dreary brick or quarry tile floor can be wiped with tan, brown and red shoe polish to bring about an instant revival and give the floor a prettier hue. Smear the different coloured polishes on with a rag, then rub them in well with a soft cloth until you achieve the desired effect. To protect the colour, finish with a couple of coats of polyurethane varnish.

This treatment also works well on concrete slabs. After smearing with polish, use a chisel to gouge out pits and wear marks in a suitably random pattern and the effect can end up looking like well-aged paving stones.

Sealed in a Flash

If the concrete floor is smooth and in one piece, you could seal it first and then paint it. Because the concrete tends to absorbs some of the paint, the final result is usually a soft, chalky version of the chosen colour, but remember that the finishing coats of polyurethane will darken the effect.

SIMPLE REVIVALS

Unless your wooden floor looks as though it is almost worn through, miraculous revivals can be brought about in just a day or two.

Scraping or sanding the floor boards down to the natural wood, and then either bleaching them or simply polishing – whichever makes the best of them – is the easiest approach, before protecting your work with an optional coat of polyurethane. You may also want to experiment with stains, dyes and inks.

But, regardless of what end result you are aiming to achieve it is of fundamental importance that you prepare the floor properly first. Short cuts at this stage usually result in more work later on, so it is definitely worth taking some trouble to get it right.

Sanding – Do It Yourself!

Some simple guidelines make scraping or sanding the floor easier if you decide to do the work yourself:

- ► If hiring a drum sander and a hand-held rotary sander (to finish off the edges) from a hardware store or machine-hire company, make sure that you are given a clear demonstration of how to use the machines before you leave the store
- ► Before you start, ensure that there are no nails or other obstacles sticking up from the floor
- ► Move as much furniture out of the room as you can
- ► Seal all cupboards and drawers with masking tape in order to protect the contents from dust
- ► Always wear goggles and a dust mask when you sand
- ► When you have achieved the required smoothness, vacuum up all of the dust and debris and then mop the floor with a mixture of one part vinegar to four parts water
- ► Allow the floor boards to dry out completely before applying any kind of finish or protective coating
- ► For a very tough protective finish you will need to apply at least two coats of polyurethane varnish

Bleached and Beautiful

For most floors, ordinary household bleach will be strong enough for this task, but for a very white effect it may be necessary to use industrial-strength bleach. With chemicals of this kind you must follow the manufacturer's instructions to the letter and always work in a well-ventilated room.

After sanding and washing, scrub the bleach into the floor. Leave it for about a quarter of an hour and then rinse it off with clean, warm water. Repeat the process until you achieve the required shade and then neutralize the floor with a half-and-half solution of vinegar and water before rinsing once again with clean water.

Lightly sand the floor again, vacuum, damp mop thoroughly, then apply two or three coats of polyurethane.

Perfect Polyurethane

This is the indispensable finish for almost all decorative treatments. It is hard, durable and water resistant, but bear in mind that it also tends to darken the surface somewhat. On large areas, apply with a roller and then go over the wet surface with a dry brush to eliminate any bubbles.

If you are polyurethaning a newly sanded floor, you should first use a sealer coat made from a half-and-half mixture of polyurethane and white spirit. Allow it to dry for at least 24 hours and then apply at least two coats of undiluted polyurethane, again allowing the requisite 24 hours in between each coat. Leave the surface alone for two days, then apply two coats of paste wax, polishing up each coat with an electric floor polisher. Once again, you should always make sure that you are working in a well-ventilated area to avoid the build up of dangerous fumes.

LEFT *Boards that have been bleached and sealed look very elegant, particularly with white walls.*

OPPOSITE ABOVE *Carefully marking out a chequerboard pattern using different toned stains can transform ordinary floor boards.*

OPPOSITE BELOW *Stripping, sanding, polishing and sealing brings floor boards up to a good-looking state.*

PAINT IT! STAIN IT!

Paint is the ultimate disguiser of cracked, chipped and otherwise unsatisfactory floors. It is easily the most outstanding reviver for battered surfaces and certainly the cheapest.

You could either cover the surface with tough, durable floor or yacht paint, or try something a little more ambitious with ordinary household paint – either oil- or water-based paint can be used since it will be protected by two or three coats of polyurethane – as this gives you a much wider choice of colours and more scope to create your own designs.

Coloured stains, inks and fabric dyes can all be used to very great effect on a well-prepared floor. Pigmented oil stains mixed with mineral spirits or turpentine seep into the wood rather slowly and so are easier for the amateur to control than the water- or alcohol-based versions which dry more quickly.

Plotting the design

For the very best results, designs should be worked out properly on graph paper, then transferred to a grid marked out on the floor:

- Mark out a grid on the floor with a metal ruler and a stick of chalk or charcoal; count out the same number of squares on graph paper
- Number the squares, both on the floor and on the graph paper
- Work out the design on the graph paper, then transfer it to the floor, square by square, using chalk or charcoal
- Use an awl to score the pattern into the floor for a crisper finish

Paint Magic

Use one colour at a time, completing the whole pattern before allowing it to dry and adding more coats to deepen the colours where necessary. When you are satisfied with the effect and the paint is completely dry, give the floor at least two coats of polyurethane.

Finally, finish off the floor with two or three coats of liquid wax and an electric floor polisher.

Instant Solutions: Stains and Dyes

Oil-based stains should be left on the floor for about ten minutes before the excess can be wiped off with a soft cloth. Do not attempt to add a second coat of stain until the first has dried completely. Each subsequent coat of stain deepens the colour of the wood – but remember that the final protective coat of polyurethane will darken the surface even further.

Inks and fabric dyes are comparatively easy to use and come in an interesting range of colours. You will need less water for fabric dyes than the manufacturer recommends for textiles: they should be applied with a rag, sponge or brush.

Whatever stain, ink or dye you use, you can use different shades or tones to create different effects, such as parquetry, marquetry, chequerboard patterns, stencils and any other design you care to try.

BELOW Narrow floor boards painted in a chequerboard design 'expand' the space in a small country entrance hall.

OPPOSITE A sinuous pattern has been stencilled on to the sanded floor of this Italian room, then stained in shades of pale grey.

COVER-UPS

Any floor covering – whether it be luxurious deep-pile carpet, a small densely patterned rug, wall-to-wall matting or a painted oilcloth – adds interesting colour and texture to a room.

If you decide you want a wall-to-wall effect, choose between the real softness of carpeting, or a crisper look with coir, sisal or rush matting. This type of matting is generally much cheaper than carpet, and provides an excellent background for a disparate collection of rugs and furniture.

Antique and modern rugs add a decorative accent to the plainest rooms, but can be expensive so look out for bargains at sales, auctions and craft fairs. Alternatively, you could paint your own floor cloth – choose from traditional geometric patterns, *trompe l'oeil* painting or simple abstract designs.

Magic Carpet

- If you have your heart set on carpet, you should get the most expensive you can possibly afford for hard-wear areas such as stairs, corridors and living rooms; cheap carpet in these areas is a false economy, as it wears quickly and will have to be replaced
- You can get away with less expensive carpeting in rooms such as bedrooms and cloakrooms as they receive less traffic than other areas
- Before you spend half your budget on expensive floor coverings, explore the possibilities of getting good carpet at factory sales where 'seconds' are sold – often with flaws that are indiscernible to the lay person's eye – at a fraction of the retail cost
- Also investigate speciality carpet retailers, which occasionally may have good-value off-cuts and returns at prices considerably lower than normal

ABOVE An expanse of herringbone coir matting lines this hallway, providing a handsome, hard-wearing floor covering which is a good foil for any mix of furniture.

RIGHT The beautifully patterned, flat woven carpet in this distinguished dining room enhances the dark modern furniture, providing warmth in a room that might otherwise appear rather gloomy and oppressive.

Instant Floor Art

Pieces of painted canvas used on the floor instead of rugs are enjoying a timely revival. They can be decorated with any sort of design, but even the least artistically gifted person can paint a piece of canvas with a plain dark ground colour and a plain border in a contrasting colour.

- ► You need primed artists' canvas (allow an extra 4 cm [1½ in] around the edge of the finished rug size), emulsion or latex paint, a large paintbrush or cheap sponge brushes, a pencil, ruler and good quality masking tape
- ► Lay the canvas flat on the floor and pencil in a line 4 cm (1½ in) from each side (this will be turned under later to make the finished edging)
- ► Then pencil in another border all around the edge and cover the lines with masking tape
- ► Paint the centre ground of the cloth, and then paint the border
- ► Wait until the paint dries and then give second or third coats if necessary
- ► When dry, apply two or three coats of polyurethane
- ► When the polyurethane is dry, turn the canvas over and gently fold over the 4 cm (1½ in) border
- ► Snip off a triangular piece of canvas from each corner to allow the canvas to lie flat
- ► Weigh the border down with weights and when it seems flat, turn it over again. If the paint has cracked slightly, touch it up with a small paint brush
- ► The floorcloth lasts longer given a fresh coat of polyurethane each year

It's a Great Idea...

- ► Dye shabby carpets or matting – this works best with pale-coloured carpets
- ► Car spray paint works wonderfully on vegetable-fibre matting and leaves a good crisp finish if you apply it using stencil cut-outs or masking tape
- ► Door matting can be bought off the roll, so it can be used to line a whole hallway – it's also a good soundproofer

A vividly coloured rug with a distinctive modern look can provide a very useful and unusual focal point. It can also draw attention away from flawed flooring.

STRONG *AND* STYLISH

If you have a hard floor – whether in wood or concrete – which needs complete, expensive resurfacing treatment, the most obvious solution is to cover it up.

Instead of carpets and rugs, consider a hard-wearing linoleum, vinyl or rubber floor covering. If you have not looked at this kind of flooring recently, no doubt you will be pleasantly surprised by the vast range of colours, patterns and even *faux* finishes now available. Even if you eschew the high-tech look associated with synthetic flooring, there are still plenty of other, softer-looking varieties to choose from.

Alternatively, you may be stuck with a floor covered in badly marked and stained linoleum which you are unable to change, but there are still quick and relatively simple ways of improving its appearance.

First Aid for Floors

Synthetic flooring is durable but prone to stains and scuff marks. Here are some proven cleaning methods:

- Dilute washing soda will bring up the surface colour of linoleum
- Emulsion floor polish will remove scuff marks from vinyl or linoleum
- Waxy marks, such as from crayons, will disappear if rubbed with a little silver metal polish
- Always use 'soft' cleaners. Abrasive cleaners damage flooring
- A 'tired' black-and-white chequerboard floor can be revived by replacing just the white tiles

Quick Revivals

If your kitchen or bathroom is covered in old linoleum, there are two different approaches you can take.

- If it is in fairly good condition with an attractive pattern or colour and simply in need of sprucing up, clean it (see right) before polishing or sealing it; ask at a good hardware store for advice on the kind of sealant you should use
- For a really economical 'new' floor, simply give it a coat of paint. Use ordinary semigloss paint and seal with polyurethane, or buy the special liquid linoleum paints available in a wide range of colours for use, in fact, on almost any surface

ABOVE Stud rubber flooring neatly anchors a streamlined white scheme.

Synthetic Selection

Linoleum, once a thin substitute for other forms of flooring, is now thick, glossy and durable; rubber was first used as an industrial flooring but is increasingly used in domestic interiors; vinyl is an excellent all-purpose material for kitchens, bathrooms and any area that receives a lot of traffic. All of these materials come in either sheet or tile form; if you are considering laying it yourself, you should probably opt for vinyl as it is easier to handle.

The smallest standard vinyl tile size is 23 cm (9 in) square, but ask the retailer if pre cut, self adhesive 21 cm (6 in) tiles are available: they are more effective in masking any irregularities in the floor surface and are more easy to handle, even if you have never attempted this kind of job before.

Be adventurous and choose an eye-catching colour combination such as grey and white, green and cream, or two shades of the same colour – such as two blues or two reds. Lay them in a chequerboard design, stripes, randomly or with a decorative border about 5 cm (2 in) out from the edge of the floor.

OPPOSITE Vinyl tiles form a diamond pattern and make a narrow hall seem wider and lighter.

BELOW An under-table 'rug' of dark-stained cork is inset into a plain surround.

Instant Solution:
NATURAL FIBRES

Nubbly sisal makes an inexpensive rug for a large area. In this bedroom, it creates an interesting textural contrast with the tiled floor. Matting of any sort, whether it be sisal, coir or seagrass, is a practical choice, being an excellent unifier, easily available and durable. ABOVE

Instant Solution:
FLOORCLOTHS

Painted canvas oilcloths have slipped in and out of popularity on both sides of the Atlantic ever since the eighteenth century. This ambitious and colourful design contrasts richly with the dark wood and shades. Floorcloths can be as simple or as complicated as you wish. RIGHT

Instant Solution:
MIXED PATTERNS

A pleasantly eclectic combination of narrow rugs and runners cover this parquet floor. ABOVE

Instant Solution:
PAINTED STAIRCASE

In this bold treatment, the banisters and runners are painted a deep blue, and treads are stripped back to their natural wood. LEFT

Instant Solution:
BLUE AND WHITE

Broad stripes in soft blue and off-white are painted on an old, narrow-boarded floor. FAR LEFT

WALLS WIZARDRY

The enormous range of available paint techniques and effects has never been so varied or so exciting

INSTANT TRANSFORMER

Paint techniques are not difficult to master – even the amateur can create stunning effects with imaginative use of colour.

Try experimenting with your chosen colours, applying them to part of the wall or to a large piece of lining paper which you can pin to the wall. Allow yourself time to get used to the colour, notice how it changes throughout the day and how it combines with your floor treatment and soft furnishings. But do not despair if you find that you have made a mistake – in the worst event, you can always paint it over. This thought should give you the courage to be bold and try new and unusual schemes.

It is important to assess carefully the condition, proportion and shape of the rooms before you make any decisions as to what sort of effects you want to achieve and what sort of paint you should use. If you feel daunted by the many different kinds of paint available, go to a good paint store where the retailer will be able to advise you. If you want to try one of the many paint methods fashionable now, consult a good paint techniques manual and test your technique first on a primed board.

Preparation Pays

Paint is normally the easiest and quickest solution for any instant transformation but, to be really effective, it looks best when applied to walls that are in good condition.

- ► Seek professional advice on dealing with any dampness, dry rot or condensation – these are problems that take time to resolve and can be expensive
- ► You can fill small cracks and ridges yourself with liquid plaster, smoothed with sandpaper, and covered with good quality lining paper to ensure a professional finish
- ► If walls are in a very poor condition, they may need to be completely re-plastered or covered with plaster-board (sheet-rock) for a smooth finish
- ► If plastered, they must be allowed time to dry out thoroughly before decoration
- ► Remember, good quality raw plaster can look spectacular if left unpainted. Seal with a matt varnish for protection

Fabulous Glazes

Glazing, which involves adding a transparent film of colour to the wall surface, is a great interior decorators' favourite, as it can transform otherwise quite plain walls.

- ► Commercial glaze or glazing liquid can be bought from good paint stores and you can either get the shop to tint it to the colour of your choice, or you can try tinting it yourself with universal tinting colours (available from artists' supply stores) or ordinary artists' oil paints. You will need much less glaze than paint for a room since glaze is thinner
- ► If you decide to keep the glaze within the same range of colours as the base coat, the result will be a delicately modified and deepened version of the base. If it is from a contrasting colour group, but of an equal intensity, or if you put a darker colour over a lighter one, the result will be an entirely different colour – with the bonus of added translucency. For example, a dark grey glaze over a Moroccan red base will give the appearance of Moroccan leather; a sienna brown glaze over deep green will create a beguiling shade of terracotta, and a deep green glaze over a lighter green base will result in a glorious jade
- ► Once again, a final coat of polyurethane will harden the surface and make it look somewhat 'antiqued'

OPPOSITE ABOVE *Bright white paint on a staircase, banisters and walls can be used to transform a previously gloomy stairwell, making the most of all the natural light available.*

OPPOSITE BELOW *Soft, aqueous paint is edged by a slim fillet of red, subtly defining the differences between a dining room and a kitchen.*

BELOW *Painting tongue-and-groove walls a gleaming duck-egg blue turns an awkward cabin-like space into a pleasant dining room.*

OVER THE TOP

You may not be able to give your walls a completely new treatment, but there are still plenty of ways in which you can revitalize them.

It is possible to generate a fresh look without going to the trouble of stripping them right back to the original plaster. Many of the treatments outlined here can be carried out on a less-than-perfect wall surface, so they are ideal if you are going to be moving house fairly shortly, or if you want a stylish stop-gap to tide you over until you get around to a complete redecoration.

Paint Tricks

- If you like the appearance of benign neglect, play up shabby painted or papered walls with a couple of coats of matt polyurethane. This will yellow and age them nicely
- For a tailored look paint a border or even a double border under the cornice, if there is one, or just below ceiling height if there is not
- Or paint a border around the edge of doors, window frames and above the skirting boards (baseboards)
- Transform a room lined with knotty wood pine by painting the walls with a special primer designed to cover all the knots and markings (which, otherwise, will eventually show through) then apply at least two coats in your chosen colour

Grand Effects

Add character to a room by painting the woodwork in a contrasting colour. Dark colours, such as navy blue and bottle green, can look surprisingly good, particularly when set off by white walls. For an even quicker – and subtler – transformation rub a coloured wax crayon into the existing woodwork. For the best results, use a darker crayon over a lighter wood. Polish up with a cloth.

ABOVE RIGHT Exposed brickwork is given a couple of coats of gloss paint to reflect the light in this light and airy bedroom.

LEFT Paint treatments are not restricted to walls – try them on floors, furniture and baths.

ABOVE Chair rails have been painted in contrasting colours to add definition to these interconnecting rooms which are full of architectural interest.

Instant Solution:
VIRTUE IN HEIGHT

In this small, high bedroom, the stencilled wall painting, towering four-poster and white bed linen all make a virtue out of height. LEFT

Instant Solution:
STENCIL IT

Elaborately stencilled walls – featuring citrus trees and draperies – transform this turn-of-the-century room into an excellent approximation of an orangerie, or winter garden room. The painted chair rail has the effect of lowering the apparent height of the ceiling. BELOW

Instant Solution:
BLUE HARMONY

The clever use of a deep blue-grey painted on matchboarded walls and doorway, combined with toile de Jouy *seat covers, gives an otherwise plain room a somewhat French appearance.* LEFT

Instant Solution:
JAZZY COLOURS

A pale buttery yellow on the lower walls is used with powder blue on the ceiling, upper walls, and shelves and a thin, red 'picture rail' line. This house demonstrates with what ease soft, 'comfortable' colours that have an affinity with each other can be rendered exciting when combined in less conventional ways. OPPOSITE

LUXURY ON A BUDGET

Such a vast array of wallcoverings is now available to the decorator – many of them relatively inexpensive and designed to be simple for the novice to use – that the most difficult problem is knowing what sort of covering to choose.

As well as wallpapers (many with co-ordinating borders), there are felts, flannels, hessians (burlaps), velvets, linens and close-woven cottons, all specially backed for ease of application. Added to this, it must be remembered that by the simple expedient of either battening, stapling, sticking or hanging, you can use almost any fabric to decorate your walls.

Cloth Bound

Muslin, dotted Swiss, or lengths of printed cotton bought in sales, or any other fabric bought cheaply, can be suspended from a rod and caught back over doors and windows. Calico and thin canvas can be bought from artists' supplies stores and make good coverings.

You can also stretch the fabric across the walls and staple it on, covering the staplemarks with a braid, a length of the same fabric, picture framing, or painted moulding. This treatment is a speedy way to make the least architecturally distinctive room look distinguished.

An original fabric wallcovering can be made with sample squares of felt bought from a sewing supplies shop, or from felt suppliers. Stick them onto the wall (applying fabric paste to the wall first), in a chequerboard design either in two colours, or in a rainbow selection, making sure that they butt up well to each other.

Wall-to-Wall

- Take advantage of the luxurious feel of expensive wallpapers and fabrics without spending an enormous price, simply by dividing them up
- Buy one or two rolls of an expensive paper and use it in panels surrounded by a paper border or by lengths of moulding
- Or cut figures or motifs out of a roll or two of expensive paper, and stick them on to the wall, or trace or paint on more formal patterns. Finish with a coat of matt polyurethane for a hardened, instantly 'antiqued' look
- One good solution is to hang high-quality lining paper and then paint it with random patterns. You can simply spatter on paint or airspray it, or let splotches dribble down for some abstract effects. Masking tape, however, should not be used on lining paper as it will pull up the paint underneath with disastrous results
- Rolls of *faux* finish wallpaper can be made to look like the most expensive, expert paint treatment if you give them a coat of semigloss polyurethane, or glaze them, then seal with polyurethane

The Simple Answer: Paper Lining

Contact paper, for drawer and shelf lining, can be used as wallpaper if given a couple of protective coats of polyurethane. It also looks good in alcoves or around fireplaces in place of missing slips or tiles.

RIGHT *'Dragged' cobalt blue* faux *finish paper in this hallway makes a rich and sumptuous background for the handsome pieces of furniture.*

BELOW RIGHT *By making walls, ceiling and furnishings all white this small dining space with its dramatic uplighter is made to appear substantially more spacious. Decorated with darker colours, the room would certainly feel much more cramped for space.*

OPPOSITE *Here, the striped wallpaper is instrumental in adding a period flavour to a featureless modern room. Remember, contemporary architecture does not have to have contemporary furnishings to match.*

BELOW *A 'marbled' dado, dark chair rail and terracotta walls – complete with Greco panels – give an exotic air to a formerly ordinary room.*

PAPER PERK-UPS

If you do not want to spend too much money on re-wallpapering (or painting), or have papering that is in good condition, but dull, there are various things you can do to perk up the existing walls.

Quite apart from adding appropriate patterned paper borders, thin strips of gilt or mahogany, picture framing, painted mouldings, or lengths of grosgrain or velvet ribbons will finish off walls and make them look more distinguished. There are a host of more unusual interior decorator's techniques for you to choose from, for every room in the house.

Paper Chase

Thin, cheap wallpaper can be made to look much more expensive and interesting by over-painting with a coat of matt polyurethane varnish. Alternatively, you could apply to the wallpaper a plain or tinted glaze which you can easily make yourself.

Cover a wallpaper that looks tired and old, especially if it has a fairly plain pattern such as a tight miniprint or a geometric design, with a useful tinted glaze, too. The effect will be to make it appear more translucent and 'antiqued' rather than shabby – but do test a small, inconspicuous area first to make sure colours do not run.

Beautiful Borders

If redecorating or re-treating a whole room seems excessive, why not try making a difference simply by applying a border? For example, a border on its own will make an enormous difference to a plain painted room, either just under the ceiling and/or above the skirting boards (baseboards), or used all around door-frames and windows as well.

If you cannot find a border you like, simply buy one roll of striped paper (and the stripes do not have to be plain – they can be clusters of flowers, posies or garlands in striped formation instead) and cut it up in lengths and use as borders.

An Instant Disguise

- In a room with fairly plain painted or papered walls, a *faux* finish in either paint or paper is an excellent way to improve the decorative quality in a very short space of time
- Consider making a print room, so popular in England in the eighteenth and early-nineteenth centuries and now revived again. All this requires is a collection of prints, preferably black and white (you could use good photocopies, aged slightly with watercolour paints), some suitable borders for frames, ribbons and decorative cords.

  Have a hanging or placement plan worked out before the final glueing. Suitable colours for the walls might be 'dirty' yellow or maroon. The prints can be stuck straight on to the wall and then given appropriate paper border 'frames'. The whole effect should be finished off with paper ribbons and bows, which can be bought ready to cut out for just such a purpose. When all is in place, give the prints and walls a coat of varnish or polyurethane to age them and keep them well-preserved

LEFT Inexpensive, figured cotton cloths are used here to great effect to cover the walls and to create bed and window treatments in a room that has an Anglo-Indian feel.

OPPOSITE Black-and-white prints turn a reading room into a learned haven. Trompe l'oeil *tassels complete the scheme.*

DUCK EGGS
FRESH DAILY
SOLD HERE

Instant Solution: DOOR COVERS

An Indian cotton bedspread has been cut out and used to form a striking frame for an Eastern-looking arched door. This is a clever way to create instant definition between two white-walled rooms. LEFT

Instant Solution: LATERAL THINKING

Matchstick (pinoleum) blind material has been used to interesting effect in this living room. This inexpensive material is simply stapled to battens attached to the wall. BELOW

Instant Solution: WOODEN DADO

A dado (wainscoting) of tongue-and-groove knotty pine can be quickly installed to create a durable wall surface. Here, it has a dual purpose defining the dining area in the corner of a hallway. OPPOSITE ABOVE

Instant Solution: GARDEN TRELLIS

Squared-off trellis provides interestingly textured walls and turns this small terrace into an extra and elegant dining space. It can also be used for its traditional purpose – as a plant support – bringing all the delights of the outdoors into the living room, as well as disguising an uninspiring view. OPPOSITE BELOW

FABRIC COVER-UPS

Fabric can be the simplest and most stylish method of revitalizing an existing scheme or creating a new one

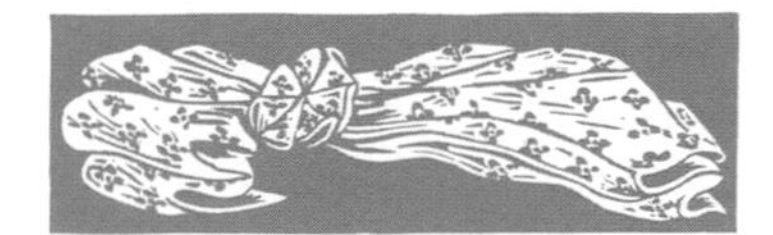

*A*BOVE *A softly gathered Austrian blind on the shorter window behind the bed matches the fullness of the long curtains without trailing untidily. Blinds or short drapes are preferable for windows that have either a bed or a sofa in front of them.*

WAYS WITH WINDOWS

Windows do not have to be oddly shaped to be difficult to treat. Take, for example, the dilemma caused by graceful arched windows.

Do you follow the arch with a fixed curved track to show off its line – and, inevitably, lose valuable light in the daytime because the curtains meet in the middle however well they are looped back at the sides? Or do you set a rod or track well above the window so the arch is visible and the light unrestricted, but sacrifice the shape of the arch when the curtains are drawn at night? Some people fix splendid arched pelmets or valances above the arch and beneath it hang curtains or drapes pulled to the sides. If you use fabric blinds a shaped section will hang permanently within the arch itself. Translucent, light cotton Austrian or festoon blinds are one answer if the view outside is not too spectacular. Another is to use Venetian or the translucent double-pleated Duette blinds with a fixed top to filter the light. Finally, a sheer curtain could be draped to one side and tied back. Or, if there is no need for a cover up, you could leave the window completely bare.

This one example demonstrates the plethora of choices open to those with less conventionally shaped windows. By all means, be practical, but trust your imagination and intuition and you may come up with a highly original solution.

Winning Window Solutions

- Windows that seem too narrow for their height need to look wider, so use a heading wider than the window and hang curtains or drapes on either side
- Windows that are too wide for their height, or too short, can look taller if long curtains are hung way above the top of the window, and the gap filled with a deep pelmet or valance
- Curtains that meet in the middle and tie back at either side reduce the apparent window width
- French windows, and sliding glass doors can be treated as normal long windows if they open outwards or slide
- If they open inwards, the rail or rod should be way above and beyond the windows or doors so that they are not obstructed by the fabric
- Alternatively, fix curtains directly on to the doors. They should be made of translucent fabrics such as voile or lace
- The best way to treat bay windows with window seats is to install Roman, roller, Austrian or festoon blinds or shades that stop short of the seat
- To soften the effect, have full (not skimpy) fixed drapes at the side – hanging straight, perhaps puddling slightly on the ground, or looped back with tie-backs
- Bay windows without window seats could have much the same treatment – always using full-, not sill-, length coverings – with full length shades and dress curtains, or curtains on a curved track, with nets or voiles if you want privacy by day
- If the view is good and there is no problem with privacy, leave beautiful old windows alone, exaggerating the frame if you like by either stripping and waxing the wood, or staining it, or painting it a contrasting colour to the room
- If the windows have shutters in working condition, either strip and wax them, or try staining, painting or stencilling them
- If privacy is a problem and the view dreary, hang rather simple, but sumptuous drapes on plain poles, looped back to show the frames
- Or use yards and yards of white muslin, draped around the pole and folding on to the floor

Remember . . .

Heat loss is usually the major problem with large windows or walls of glass, so use full length curtains or draperies both lined and interlined.

- Windows set close together, even unmatched ones, are best treated as one with a long pole or track, and/or pelmet or valance determined by the height of the taller window
- Sometimes one very large curtain or drape looped back to the side of the furthest window can look handsome

High Lights

- Dormer windows, sloping attic windows and skylights all tend to be rather small, so do not restrict what light they do let in. Either leave them bare, or use hinged curtain tracks to pull back against the wall during the day and snap back over the windows at night
- Sloping windows can have sheer fabrics fixed to rods or poles, top and bottom, as can skylights, or you can fix Venetian or mini-blinds to both with special fixings
- Stained glass windows, half-moon, crescent, round and other unusually shaped windows are best left uncovered, or use a roller blind, wider than the window and set above it so as not to destroy the decorative effect by day

'Warm' Looks

Cold-looking rooms will be enormously warmed by using a warm-looking rose or apricot or red window treatment. Try using rose-coloured linings behind other fabrics for a warm, roseate glow on much the same principle. Thin roller blinds with a yellowish tint will certainly make any room seem much warmer.

OPPOSITE ABOVE *Use a softly draped curtain, looped to one side with a metal clasp, to show off tall windows. Here, the curtain filters the light and serves to balance the room's striking, powerful art objects.*

OPPOSITE LEFT *Carefully pleated blinds over a row of deeply recessed windows let in the light but provide privacy.*

Instant Solution: FROM BEDSPREAD TO DECORATIVE DISPLAY

Doors are frequently overlooked when planning a decorative scheme. Too often a coat or two of paint is thought to be all that is needed when decorating, but doors can be a positive force, and one way of giving them character and individuality is to frame them in draperies. Here, a fine fringed and crocheted linen bedspread, cut up and hung on loops from a narrow wooden batten, is used to stunning effect as a softening frame for a panelled door. An over-fussy look is avoided by painting the door a gloss white and the surrounding wooden walls a greenish-white. BELOW

Instant Solution: CRISP WHITE SHEETS

A quick, easy and, above all, inexpensive method of dressing windows, is to use plain, white cotton bed sheets. Here, single sheets have been adapted to elegantly frame each of the four identical picture windows. Held back in position by brass embrasses, *these elegant curtains are perfectly suited to the quality of light and style of furnishing; they help disguise the hard angles of the two, almost mirror-image, rooms. The swagged semi-circular valances, also made from sheets, have been tied in rosettes to the curtain pole, adding to the softening and sophisticating effect in both rooms.* RIGHT

Instant Solution:
KEEP IT SIMPLE

Window treatments do not have to be ornate to be effective, and nor do they have to be expensive. Here, simplicity is the key to this stylish solution. Printed blue-and-white cotton has been given the simplest of headings – looped over a wooden pole – and the most basic wooden bosses hold the drapery away from the window. The curtains are unlined, enhancing the sense of light and space in what could easily be, with a less sympathetic decorative scheme, a claustrophobic landing. The whole scheme is restricted to two colours, the blue picked up in the walls and oriental jar, and the white used on the floor and chair. LEFT

Instant Solution:
BLANKET COVER-UP

Bright woollen blankets, complete with fringes, have been simply looped over wooden poles to make quick and visually arresting curtains. The colour scheme has been repeated in the spare decoration of the room – the vibrant red has been picked out in the thin red line painted around the whole room at picture rail height, and the shades of mauve and yellow repeated in the paintwork. The icon and battered wooden chair also share the colour scheme to unify the room. When closed, these floor-length curtains will certainly keep out any unwanted draughts in winter and also make the room warm and cosy. ABOVE

TRIMMINGS GALORE

Few things dress up a room as much as sumptuous drapery. However, the opportunity that curtains represent to make a room look well thought out is seized only rarely.

Treatments often consist of two limp pieces of fabric intended merely to maintain privacy and keep out light – without a thought being given to their decorative potential. If you have inherited unimaginative drapery that you are unable to replace, there is almost always something you can do to improve its contribution to your overall scheme.

Fabric Magic

Curtains and blinds can all be trimmed with one of the many decorative edgings now available. Curtains can be given swags and tails, fringes and pelmets.

Existing pelmets or valances can be made more elaborate with rosettes, bobbles or fringes. Fabric Roman or roller blinds can be given an extra border or trim – they can also be given a pelmet if you are seeking to achieve a grander look.

- You could sew contrasting fabric borders to the leading and bottom edges of plain fabric, or bind the edges, using grosgrain or velvet ribbon, gimp, braid or contrasting cotton fabric cut into appropriately-sized widths
- Lined curtains always look sophisticated and they need not be expensive or time-consuming to make. Choose a lightweight print or solid coloured fabric to complement your existing curtains. Use your present curtains as a template when cutting out. Sew the lining to the back of your curtains, fix a loop to the corner of the leading edge and attach it to a hook or decorative curtain boss at a suitable height on the window frame to expose the graceful contrast

Underglow

- Delicate under-curtains in silk, cotton or voile will soften the effect of the heaviest curtain treatment. White or cream are the most popular colours, but pink casts a warm glow, whereas green or blue creates a cool atmosphere in even the stuffiest of city apartments

Stencilled Designs

Plain cottons, silks, linens or linen unions can be stencilled with a border motif or even given an ambitious all-over design. You could stencil a pair of tie-backs, or decorate a strip of fabric which could be attached to the bottom of a pair of curtains. Or, you could add four stencils to the corners of each curtain.

ABOVE A deep inset border and double-corded tie-backs enliven these long velvet curtains.

TOP White muslin curtains are charmingly transformed with pink and yellow ribbons.

OPPOSITE White linen curtains and pelmet are edged with baubles and tied back by decorated cords.

Tie-Backs

The simple expedient of adding tie-backs to generously cut but otherwise undistinguished curtains can improve them immeasurably. It is important that your tie-backs are generously cut – you want them to hold the curtains gracefully, not to look like a skimpy afterthought.

- The most usual tie-backs are made either from the same material as the curtains or from another fabric in an appropriate colour. Edge them with a contrasting braid or fringe for that special polish
- Buy a selection of cords in colours taken from the curtains or room. Twist them together and loop them around the pulled-back fabric attaching them to brass hooks set at your chosen height
- You could use ready-knotted cords, with or without tassels, for a classic, period look, though this would be a more expensive solution
- A popular interior decorators' technique is to buy ½ m (½ yd) each of three plain fabrics in suitable colours and then make them into three tubes, stuffing them if you want an attractive, plump effect. The tubes are then cut in half and plaited together to make two tie-backs. Cover the ends with fabric, sew rings to the ends and attach them to brass hooks
- The simplest tie-backs of all are made from wide ribbon or beautiful silk scarves tied in luxurious bows
- You could look out for some of the brass or gilt tie-backs and bosses presently enjoying great popularity. They are available in a wide range of designs and are intended to be fixed to the walls, ready to restrain luxurious folds of fabric

It's a Great Idea...

- Spend some time experimenting with the height at which you want to attach your tie-back or boss – you may be surprised by how dramatically the chosen height can change the look of the window
- Try tying the curtains loosely with a piece of string and moving the string to different positions to see what looks best
- Stand back so that you can assess how well the curtains fall

SLIP AND LOOSE COVERS

A piece of upholstered furniture is always one of the most expensive items to replace – so revamp!

If you have a limited budget, simple loose covers can make a world of difference to a sound but otherwise uninteresting piece of furniture.

BELOW Deep, squashy sofas are loose-covered in a pretty chintz, giving the whole room a comfortable homeliness.

BOTTOM Cover cushions, table skirts, sofa and curtains with different but harmonious patterns.

OPPOSITE A shabby old armchair is given a new lease of life by artfully arranged fringed shawls and throws.

Loose and Lovely

- ► If the piece of furniture is sturdy but worn from years of use, or you are simply bored with it, loose covers in a fresh fabric will provide an instant pick-me-up. This can sometimes be quite expensive, bearing in mind the large amount of fabric needed, as well as the labour costs if you are going to employ someone else to do it
- ► It is not nearly so expensive to give an occasional or dining chair a new cover. Casually tied loose covers that fit most standard-sized chairs are now widely available through mail-order companies or from large department stores. They usually come in plain canvas or colourful ticking and are an instant brightener
- ► You can dye the covers to match the rest of your furniture, or stencil patterns on plain covers if you want a more ornate overall effect

The Easy Drape

If loose covers are going to take too big a bite out of your budget, you can freshen up a tired chair or sofa by draping it with beautiful fabric. This soft, casual look is much sought after – it is cheap, easy to do, and infinitely variable, adding instant colour and interest to any room.

Try experimenting with throws, shawls, parachute silk, rugs, pieces of interesting fabric such as good fur imitations for a luxurious look, or softly patterned chintz to add romantic appeal. Top it all by adding a few cushions in contrasting fabrics or trims. Antique fabrics are worth looking out for if you want to take the 'new' edge off a well decorated, but otherwise dull room.

It's a Great Idea...

- ► Consider sheets – they come in a huge variety of designs, from classic white to stripes, florals and polka dots. A double sheet is the perfect size to wrap around an armchair. Stretch it tightly over the back and sides, tuck it in around the seat and then knot it on either side
- ► A great deal of difference can be made to the look of a plainly upholstered piece of furniture by finishing off the bottom with fringes, edging or braid in a contrasting colour. Use fabric glue to attach it to the base of the piece

Instant Solution:
UNUSUAL BEDHEAD

A heavily patterned screen makes an unusual headboard for a plain modern bed. RIGHT

Instant Solution:
TRANSPARENT DRAPES

The fabric is put up with thumb tacks and then draped, caught and swirled. BELOW

Instant Solution:
FOUR-POSTER

Simple curtain poles attached to the ceiling beams are an easy way to create a romantic four-poster effect, separate off the bathing area of the room, and soften the effect of the brick walls. The calming look of gauzy, white cotton side-panels is a gentle contrast to the geometric rose, red and white pattern of the quilt. OPPOSITE ABOVE

Instant Solution:
QUILTED

Pretty, faded pink-and-white quilts are used to cover the floor, table and window, as well as to dress the bed. The bed's base is swamped in quilts, and another is gathered up to form a soft, sumptuous bedhead. Never use beautiful old heirloom quilts as floor coverings – they should be used only over a bed or where they will not be subjected to heavy wear. OPPOSITE BELOW

Instant Solution:
ORIENTAL COVERS

Follow tradition and cover a table with a rug as they did in the seventeenth century. LEFT

Instant Solution:
BEAUTIFUL PAISLEY

Tables look particularly handsome when covered with cloths – the more exotic and idiosyncratic the better. Here, the richly coloured paisley shawl is very elegant against pale ochre-painted walls and a display of Victoriana. BELOW

Instant Solution:
WHITE ON WHITE

Few things look better than elegant, simple white cotton used to dress a table. Here, a plain undercloth is covered in a gracefully swagged overcloth. OPPOSITE ABOVE

Instant Solution:
SIMPLE COLOURS

A paisley-bordered wool shawl looks particularly fine flung over a trailing undercloth of toile de Jouy. OPPOSITE BELOW LEFT

Instant Solution:
BRIGHT PATTERNS

This striking tablecloth adds colour and pattern to a subdued room. OPPOSITE BELOW RIGHT

alea

BLIND FAITH

Fabric curtains and blinds with their attendant accessories are clearly not the only way to dress up a window.

Quite apart from dressing up the frame and surround, the choice of window coverings is extensive. Choose from – among other things – wooden shutters, pinoleum or matchstick, bamboo, Venetian and paper blinds, screens, grilles, glass shelves, and painted, stained or etched glass to create simple, effective window treatments with the least amount of fuss.

Attention Getter

- If you have a stunning view, you could treat the window frame as though it were a picture frame
- For a good view and deeply recessed windows, lining the recesses with mirror will add extra glimpses of the view as well as giving the extra bonus of more sparkle and refracted light
- Screens placed on either side of a short window create the impression of a longer, more distinguished window. Treat the screens in a variety of ways – paint them in a plain colour, cover them with *trompe l'oeil* scenes or pad them with fabric

Sun Block

- If a view is dreary, ordinary paper or pinoleum blinds can be painted or stencilled – for a quick and easy solution, try using car spray paint
- Louvred wooden shutters always look handsome, adding crisp lines and architectural interest to plain windows. Either leave them natural or paint them in a suitable colour
- Consider covering up the window completely. Glue Japanese rice paper to artists' stretching bars attached to the inside of the window frame to make a screen that will allow sunlight into the room while blocking an ugly view
- If you have a window with a deep recess, one of the most successful treatments is to fill the window with three or four glass shelves upon which you can stand a collection of coloured glass objects, plants, pewter or anything that looks good against the light

Continental Rhythm

Ordinary windows looking out on a less-than-ravishing scene can be given continental charm by fixing a striped canvas awning above the window and colourful window boxes at sill level. Conceal outdoor lights beneath the awning to illuminate the scene at night. Before embarking on this scheme, however, you should ensure that you are not contravening any local by-laws, or your leasing agreement.

BELOW LEFT Glass shelves stretched between window frames make an ideal display area for a collection of striking blue bulb vases.

BELOW RIGHT An Art-Nouveau-style stained glass panel fixed across a deeply recessed window obviates the need for a curtain.

OPPOSITE This easy-to-make blind has been created by looping ribbons around a straight piece of fabric and tying them at the bottom.

FURNITURE DISGUISES

Paint and fabric are instant and inexpensive disguisers for and enhancers of all sorts of furniture and furnishings

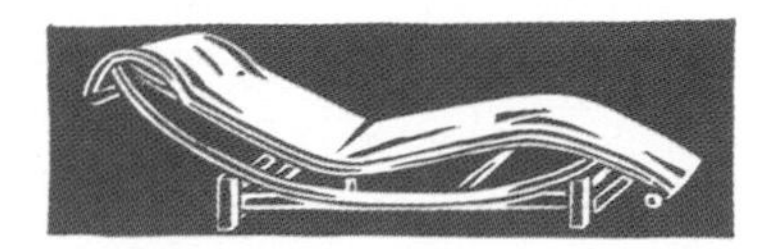

FOUND OR INHERITED?

Happily, furnishings usually look all the better for being put together with some care and thought over a period of years. Buying everything *en masse* often creates an atmosphere like a chain hotel room, without an ounce of the charm or style of a room that has slowly evolved and matured along with its inhabitants.

Fortunately, with a certain amount of effort and a lot of patience, all kinds of second-hand furniture discoveries, family hand-me-downs, whitewood and unfinished furniture and even street finds can be given a face lift. As with floors, furniture can be stripped, stained, painted, stencilled, distressed, marbled and covered in different ways, depending upon the piece and the use you want to put it to. It may be time consuming, but the pride you can take in creating your own unique pieces of furniture is certainly worth the effort.

Restoring or re-finishing a battered but sound piece of antique furniture is certainly an art and, unless you are prepared to put some effort into the study of furniture restoration, it is probably better to have it done professionally if you can afford it.

Instant Chair

Attractive and comfortable seating has to be one of the main priorities for anyone setting up home. It can also take a huge bite out of your budget. However, with a little imagination and ingenuity, homely but plain chairs can contribute to the style quotient in any room.

- ► After priming and undercoating a sturdy set of wooden dining chairs, you could paint half of them black and the other half white, or in three or four different colours to match the fabric of the window treatment or the wallpaper
- ► Unattractive reproduction chairs can be improved a hundredfold by *faux* lacquering them a deep glossy green or terracotta to reproduce the wonderful effect of Chinese or Pompeiian rusty red or black
- ► If your chairs have cane or rush seating that has seen better days, cover the seating area with pieces of strong plywood painted in an suitable colour; make them comfortable with squab cushions covered in a toning or contrasting fabric and tied to the back of the chair with self-coloured bows or silk ribbon

Ten Times Table

Tables are easy to cover and can be improvised using all manner of different materials.

- ► Scruffy dining and side tables, whether rectangular, round or oval, should be thought of as a useful base and then covered with a floor-length cloth
- ► Side tables and occasional tables, as well as the inexpensive and endlessly versatile cubes now available in nearly every discount furniture store, can be lacquered, covered with fabric or even wallpaper; and finished with polyurethane for maximum toughness
- ► Coffee tables, which tend to be either surprisingly hard to find or ludicrously expensive, can be made quite easily from a 2.5cm (1in) thick sheet of plate glass or perspex, cut to order with bevelled or rounded edges, and a variety of bases – from wood to concrete
- ► You could also adapt this method to make a dining table, although you will need to use a more stable base than for a coffee table. Good bases are old sewing machine or washstand bases, sawn-off tree trunks, evenly levelled off, and cut-off columns or pedestals

It's a Great Idea...

There are many different things you can use as the base of an occasional table, from the fanciful to the practical. Here are some useful suggestions:

- ► Large terracotta flower pots, either standing on their rims or on their bases; if the latter, consider filling them with pebbles or shells and using a see-through perspex top
- ► Wine crates – they may be full of wine, which will aid stability and be an inventive storage solution
- ► Milk crates can be painted a suitable colour or left bare; plastic crates are not as sturdy but are visually pleasing
- ► Old trunks look handsome, but make sure that there are no rough corners to catch on clothes
- ► Lacquered or covered cubes are convenient; they can be extended at will
- ► Piles of 'coffee table' books would be an appropriate – yet witty – visual joke

ABOVE Angular, painted furniture is softened by the blue interior of the bookcase, blue-and-white china, and pretty squab cushions. Coir matting is a suitable backdrop for the simple, clean lines of the furniture and is a cheap, hard-wearing and easy-to-lay alternative to more traditional flooring such as carpeting.

LEFT You can unite a disparate group of wooden chairs and make them more comfortable at very little cost by adding matching cushions. Here, a collection of coloured glass adds sparkle to an otherwise dark interior.

BACK TO BASICS

The eventual success of all furniture restoration or rejuvenation depends as much on careful preparation, stripping and final finishing as on any chosen decoration. It is vital that you take as much time and care as you can at this stage to ensure successful results later.

Stripping the Old

If the piece has been painted before and is now shabby, discoloured and flaking, the old paint will have to be removed before you can start on the improvement process. Paint strippers come in paste, gel or liquid form – ask the retailer which one would be best for your needs and make sure you follow the instructions on the container to the letter. If any paint remains, repeat the process. After stripping, neutralize the treated surface, as any stripper left on by accident will eat in to subsequent coats of paint, then smooth the surface down with a piece of fine sandpaper.

There are special kits available for furniture that merely needs years of old wax and dirt removed from the surface. They can save a large amount of time and are well worth the extra expense.

Adding the Shine

Furniture covered with wallpaper, or coffee table tops that you want to make as impregnable as possible, should be finished with a coat of polyurethane. Other pieces generally look much better if they are finished with an oil-based varnish (these vary in tone from pale cream to tawny yellow) and wax polish. Available in matt, eggshell, semigloss and gloss, varnishes tend to yellow the surface slightly, so choose the palest one for the palest colours.

- First, clean down the object you want to treat using a tack cloth (a cloth soaked in hot water, sprinkled with white or mineral spirits and three teaspoons of furniture oil, then wrung out well; it should be hung up to dry for half an hour and put in a screw-top jar until needed)
- Stir the varnish well, then strain it through a fine mesh (an old nylon stocking is ideal) into another receptacle. If it does not flow well, stand the container in warm water or thin it slightly with one part white or mineral spirits to two parts varnish
- Pour some of the varnish into another container, then dip your brush into the varnish; work it well into the bristles by brushing it firmly with the piece of hardboard – this helps prevent frothing. Next, dip the brush no more than 15mm (½ in) into the varnish and wipe against the inside of the container (not against the rim, as this will cause air bubbles to form in the varnish)
- Paint on the varnish with the grain of the wood then cross brush against the grain for an even effect
- For best results, apply two coats, drying thoroughly between coats
- Next, rub it down with a piece of well-moistened wet-and-dry sandpaper
- Wipe the surface with a damp cloth and, when dry, dip a large pad of fine steel wool in wax furniture polish and rub, following the grain of the wood
- When the wax dries, give it a final polish with a clean, soft cloth

---

Safety First

If you are going to use one of the powerful solvents required in some stages of furniture restoration, you should follow some basic guidelines shown here:

- Wear long-sleeved clothing and rubber gloves – wear a face mask if it says that you should do so on the container
- Work in a well-ventilated space
- Cover surrounding surfaces with a layer of newspaper or a piece of plastic

---

The pine cupboard and oak table have been stripped and waxed to bring out the natural beauty of the woods.

NEW FOR OLD

As with old and cracked walls, paint is a wonderful way of disguising less-than-perfect furniture surfaces and of transforming plain or even ugly pieces into highly original objects of envy. It is best to go through at least the primary stages of stripping and sanding the surface, but after that – give your imagination free rein!

Paint Perfect

After preparing the surface, prime it and give it an undercoat, then apply two coats of eggshell paint in the colour of your choice. When each coat is dry, sand it with fine grain garnet paper to get maximum smoothness. Wipe off all the residue with a cloth before painting again. If there are any carved surfaces, they are best rubbed down with fine steel wool. Protect the whole piece with a coat or two of regular oil varnish for a lasting finish.

Glazing looks as good on furniture as it does on walls; follow the same instructions. Use a tinted glaze over an already painted surface, or on stripped and sanded wood. Rag roll a tinted glaze over a neutral-coloured base coat; stippled or dragged effects look best applied to newer wood.

Instant Aging

Antiquing tends to work best on a piece of old, worn furniture, although it can also be tried on newer pieces if you distress the surface a little before you start.

An Easy Technique

The normal base for antiquing is an umber or earth-coloured glaze over a lighter base coat, but you could be more adventurous – use off-white over a grey base for the look of driftwood; a green base with a deep brown glaze; a blue base with a darker blue or green; a red base with a deep grey or black glaze; or a creamy white with a mid green.

'Antiquing' kits are available from speciality paint and home accessories stores, as are commercially made glazes. These may save time, but do not underestimate the great satisfaction gained from completing the project by yourself. Making your own glaze will also give you a greater range and flexibility of colour.

It is important that, before you start on your piece of furniture, you test out your colour combinations and your technique on a piece of board as near in texture as possible to the intended wood. Paint the board with a couple of coats of eggshell or semi-gloss oil-based paint and allow it to dry. Brush on the tinted glaze and as it starts drying (be prepared – it will dry very quickly) take a rag, pad of wire wool or sponge and dab it off. The remaining residue will leave a most convincing old patina. When you feel satisfied with the colour combination and the finish and confident that you can recreate the effect, you can begin working on the real thing. Work on small areas at a time, to prevent the glaze from drying.

When the glaze is perfectly dry, give the piece a couple of coats of oil-based varnish.

ABOVE LEFT *White paint – the greatest reviver – and broadly striped cotton have made a good-looking space from very little.*

LEFT *A distressed effect can add rustic charm.*

OPPOSITE ABOVE *Gold paint can add grandeur to an otherwise undistinguished chair.*

OPPOSITE BELOW *Subtle marbling has given a completely new identity to a chest of drawers in this romantically-orientated room.*

FABRIC DISGUISES

From throwing a beautiful parachute silk cover over a scruffy sofa to making a fitted cloth for a small table, the effects you can achieve with fabric combine practicality with inventiveness.

Experiment with colour, texture and scale, and bear in mind that the simplest techniques often make the strongest statement. With the number of excellent step-by-step furnishing publications now available, there is no reason why someone with rudimentary sewing skills should not be able to make anything from simple loose covers to a dramatic dressed table.

LEFT Pushing an iron bed up against the wall, and giving it bolsters at either end, makes it look elegantly sofa-like.

BELOW Kelim rugs can be draped over armchairs, sofas and tables, creating their own interesting harmonies.

Dressing Tables

- Even the least attractive table can take on a new lease of life if given a floor-length cloth, perhaps with an overcloth for an even more luxurious effect. There are now many inexpensive, chipboard tables on the market designed to be covered in this way – shop around until you find one that is the correct size for your room. Sturdy old tables, trunks, boxes or tea-chests are also suitable for this kind of treatment
- Dining tables are usually best served by the addition of a fairly permanent heavy cloth. Cut the fabric generously so that it sweeps the ground and line and/or interline to make it more substantial and 'weighty'
- If you make several smaller overcloths at the same time, they can be changed and laundered easily
- An attractive finishing touch would be to make co-ordinating napkins from any left-over fabric you may have
- Side tables can be given a similar treatment. Cloths can be pleated or split at the sides so that they hang crisply to the floor

Occasional Tables

- Smaller, round occasional tables of the sort that are so useful in bedrooms or beside sofas can look spectacular with undercloths made from richly textured fabrics such as velvet or brocade and then draped with old quilts or shawls
- A fresher, more informal look can be achieved by replacing a luxurious undercloth with plain cotton or muslin juxtaposed with patterned chintz, stripes or checks

Just Add Trimmings

Do not forget the potential of trimmings such as braid, tassels and fringes for such cloths, as they can lift even the most modest fabrics to sumptuous heights. A particularly dramatic effect can be achieved by trimming an undercloth with a heavy fringe and then adding tassels to its four corners.

A colourful collection of striped Mexican blankets used both for cover and for cushions has transformed a single bed into a bright, eye-catching couch.

Instant Solution: FAUX FINISHES

A simple wooden table has been lifted out of the ordinary with a hand-painted faux *tortoiseshell finish, which is well protected with polyurethane. It makes a magnificent surface on which to arrange a handsome still-life with toning flowers, painting, a brass plate of spicy-smelling pomanders and a fine shawl.* BELOW

Instant Solution: CHEAP CHIC

Great style on a limited budget – the most expensive items in this pleasing living room are the cream canvas Roman blinds and long yellow-lined curtain. Furniture is cheap and chic: cottton-covered cubes – the fabric secured with a staple gun – a cloth-covered card table and two canvas directors' chairs. RIGHT

Instant Solution: FABULOUS FABRIC

Using a happy mix of patterned fabrics – florals, plaids and plains – in a good range of colours brightens up this country-style living room. The covers are bright and loose, the tablecloth reaches to the floor and cushions are piled in a comfortable heap to soften the look of stripped shutters and furniture. OPPOSITE ABOVE RIGHT

Instant Solution: KEEP IT SIMPLE

The gracious proportions and abundant natural light in this ground-floor living room are highlighted by the simple treatment – unadorned white walls, Roman blinds, floorboards stained a rich brown – and carefully chosen furniture and accessories. A glass top rests on trunks to make a coffee table. OPPOSITE BELOW RIGHT

Fitted kitchens can be expensive and time-consuming to replace, so think about giving yours a facelift instead

SCIENCE OF APPLIANCES

Your kitchen, however small or badly proportioned it may be, will probably be one of the most heavily used areas of your house and as such it needs to be well planned and functional as well as a pleasant place to spend your time.

How well equipped your kitchen will be depends entirely on your budget and how keen a cook you are, but there are a few kitchen basics to be borne in mind whatever your situation. Give some thought to what professional kitchen planners call 'the work triangle' – that is, the area linking preparation, cooking and washing-up spaces. Ideally, you should have enough space to work efficiently in each area without them being so far apart that you spend a frustrating amount of time walking between.

If you have to plan a kitchen from scratch and cannot afford to buy any appliances except the minimum cooker (stove) and refrigerator, do leave suitable gaps for appliances you think you will purchase in the future. In the meantime, the spaces can be covered with shelves, doors or curtains to provide extra storage.

Old appliances that still work well can be cheered up with a coat of epoxy varnish paint or by other paints designed specifically for such uses.

Cook Up

The choice between gas and electricity is really one of personal preference. However, unless you already have mains gas supply or you are doing a great deal of renovation work, it is probably not worth the great inconvenience that is involved in having gas laid on.

There are now so many different types of cooker or stove on the market, there is almost bound to be one to suit your particular culinary and budgetary requirements. As with all kitchen appliances, investigate the possibility of buying used goods. Antique stoves can add charm to a country kitchen.

Cooling Down

When buying refrigerators and freezers, you should give careful consideration to the number of people in your household and your cooking and eating habits.

- Do you shop every day, or once a week?
- Do you like to cook ahead, or do you prepare each meal just before you are ready to eat?
- How much space do you have: is there room for a separate freezer, or would a model that combines refrigerator and freezer be more suitable?
- Do you need any extras such as a frost-free facility, an iced-water dispenser or ice-cream maker?

Wish List

Here is a list of appliances that will make your life easier. They are not essential at first, although you might want to bear them in mind when you plan your kitchen.

- Washing machine
- Spin drier
- Dishwasher
- Microwave
- Waste-disposal unit
- Food processor
- Extractor hood

TOP Position the stove and sink opposite each other for maximum efficiency in a narrow kitchen.

LEFT Refrigerators and dish washers can be hidden behind cabinet doors.

OPPOSITE In the space between the stove and hood an iron rod holds utensils within reach.

UNIT SOLUTIONS

There is almost always something you can do to improve your kitchen, however unappealing it may look at first sight – or even however complete and well planned it seems.

We are bombarded with advertising that implies modern, built-in units are essential for an efficient kitchen, so it is easy to lose sight of the fact that they are not entirely necessary. After all, they are a comparatively modern invention – people managed for centuries with dressers or hutches, pierced cupboards, bread and plate racks and capacious old tables.

In fact, some of the most convenient kitchens consist of a series of shelves and hooks above the work surface displaying everyday utensils and ingredients within reach. The common complaints of too little space and too little storage can usually be remedied by a little ingenuity.

New Look to Old Units

- Chests of drawers, cupboards, shelves, pine cabinets and the lower half of old dressers make wonderful kitchen storage – topped with butchers' block, Formica, ceramic tiles and even marble or slate (use old slabs of marble and slate, bought from an architectural salvage company, and have them cut to fit)
- The space in between shelves and counter top could have a 60cm (2ft) run of tiles. Try creating a frieze of odd tiles – a good way to create a stunning feature for comparatively little money
- Or paste contact paper on to existing plain tiles and then finish them off with a couple of coats of polyurethane, or you could simply paint existing tiles with gloss paint, giving them an undercoat of metal primer
- If tiling is too difficult or expensive, cut hardboard to the correct size and then paint or stencil it to look like marble or proper tiles
- Ingenious cabinets can be made from sturdy wooden packing boxes: cut hardboard for dividers, and add ready-made doors and a slab top

TOP *Retain architectural interest where possible.*

LEFT *Neatly squared shelves are used for display and storage.*

OPPOSITE *Folding doors conceal kitchen shelves.*

Instant Solution: HANGING BASKETS

A hanging wire basket can be used to store all manner of items. The supports must be secured to a joist; the basket should hang over a work surface so that you can't bump your head on it. This type of feature would suit a more modern kitchen, but you could use baskets in a country kitchen. Here, fresh produce is stored away from pets and pests at ground level. For additional storage you could hang butchers' hooks from the basket which could be used for nets of fruit or vegetables, or even bunches of fresh herbs and dried flowers, to great decorative effect. RIGHT

Instant Solution: DISH RACK

A neat cupboard, which has been tucked into a small recess, is fitted with wooden slats so that it can take the maximum amount of vertically stacked dishes. Such a device crosses the threshold from functional storage to decorative display. Similarly, a collection of chopping boards is used to add interest to this corner of a small kitchen. Antique chopping boards can be found with the word 'bread' carved around the edge and are particularly attractive kitchen accessories. Glass jars, filled with pasta, rice and colourful lentils, make functional as well as decorative storage. ABOVE

Instant Solution:
HANG 'EM UP

An ingenious rack for glasses has been suspended from the ceiling in this kitchen-diner. The rack provides not only additional storage space but also serves as a break between the kitchen and dining area. A similar device could be used for bottles, perhaps with cordials inside for a colourful effect. This type of hanging storage, however, must be fixed to a joist which can carry the full weight (including the items to be stored!). ABOVE

KITCHEN FACELIFTS

Many of us have adequately equipped kitchens that are well planned and functional. But all too frequently the kitchen is neither cheerful nor inviting and needs a facelift.

If you have spent the lion's share of your budget on appliances and have very little left over for decoration, there is still a lot you can do by adapting many of the principles used in decorating the other rooms in the house. Do not feel confined by the conventions of kitchen design – some of the most striking kitchens have unusual, eye-catching details – but do bear in mind that the kind of surfaces you choose will receive a great deal of wear and tear, so make them as practical as possible.

Quick Transformations

Surfaces have to stand up well to steam, grease, smoke and the other by-products of an active kitchen.

- ► It is difficult to wash smoke and grease off walls painted with emulsions, so use gloss or oil-based eggshell paints for maximum washability. Some paint manufacturers now produce acrylic paints with a satin, easy-wipe finish and a mild fungicide to guard against bacteria
- ► If you decide on wallpaper, use a paper-backed vinyl, a vinyl-impregnated fabric paper, or a PVC wallcovering which are all easy to keep clean. Alternatively, give ordinary wallpaper a coat of eggshell or gloss polyurethane to make it more durable and longlasting
- ► Tiles are a more expensive alternative, but are easy to clean and extremely hard wearing. New tiles can be laid on top of existing ones: clean old tiles thoroughly, and score glazed tiles with a sharp tool before applying adhesive

Colour Zone

- White paint reflects light and gives a clean, fresh look to the dreariest of kitchens. Use this as a background and personalize it by displaying collections of favourite china, or adding beautifully worn pieces of kitchen furniture
- In a country-style kitchen, earth tones would impart the right atmosphere as well as looking good with displays of fruit, vegetables and herbs
- Rusty red matt paint colour-washed over a sandy colour creates a warm, cosy kitchen
- For a brighter, crisper look use yellow, blue or green combined with white
- Lighter colours are good choices for walls and work surfaces as any dirt will show immediately and can be wiped away
- Transform dull walls by rag rolling or dragging a contrasting colour over pale paint. Or use two closely related colours, such as a deep pink over pastel pink
- Stencilled borders around the door and window frames are a quick way of livening a dull kitchen. Alternatively, add a paper frieze to enliven your existing decorative scheme

TOP *A long strip of plain white formica can be used to cover up a multitude of sins.*

LEFT *Use different tiles to create a colourful effect; trim with bright paint.*

OPPOSITE *Blue paint on cabinets and mouldings gives this kitchen a cheerful uplift.*

RESURFACING

Instead of replacing your existing kitchen units there is no reason why you cannot transform them with a facelift.

A couple of coats of paint, some new hardware and perhaps some stencilled borders or motifs may be all that is needed. If cupboard fronts seem beyond repair but the main structure is solid, you can buy new doors or even cut down old shutters to fit. Worn and chipped white goods, such as refrigerators and washing machines, and even porcelain sinks can be given a more cheery look without breaking the bank. And remember, a judicious use of colour on carefully prepared surfaces will draw the eye away from the room's other unfortunate imperfections.

BELOW The use of Corian behind the units and as a worktop thoroughly updates this room.

OPPOSITE Give kitchen cabinets an instant facelift with new doors and handles.

Worktops from Scrap

A long, uninterrupted run of worktops gives a streamlined, uncluttered appearance to a kitchen. Experiment with strong, distinctive colours for a sophisticated effect. You could cover existing surfaces with hardboard and then paint them either in a solid colour or with some kind of *faux* finish, or even cover them with contact paper or wallpaper. All of these treatments should be given two or three coats of polyurethane to make them tile hard.

It is possible to find old pieces of travertine, marble or slate that might fit. If the worktop area is quite small, the quantities required may be affordable, even if bought new.

And then there is always the huge range of vinyl-covered blockboards designed specifically for kitchen work surfaces. They are available in a huge variety of designs and colours and will add instant neatness to any untidy kitchen.

Cabinet Chic

Cabinets in poor condition or those which are simply dull-looking can be given an extra spark of life with a coat of paint.

- To paint wooden cabinets, first sand them down, prime them with an undercoat and then paint them with gloss or eggshell paint
- Doors coated in a vinyl finish should be sanded with wet-and-dry sandpaper before being primed and painted
- For added protection from culinary drips and spills, give the newly painted units a final coat of polyurethane
- You can use car spray paint for an instant finish. This is a particularly good way to add stencilled motifs to your cabinets. The same motif can be repeated on tiled splash-backs, curtains and woodwork for a harmonious effect

Priming the Porcelain

If you are lucky enough to have a deep, old-fashioned porcelain sink, even if it is in poor condition, it can be rescued by re-surfacing, either in white or a colour.

ADDITIONAL STORAGE

More than any other room in the house, the modern kitchen poses its own special storage problems. Frequently, it is either too small or poorly laid out – or both.

To combat this, look at your kitchen with an uncompromising eye. If space is at a premium, make a rule: there is no place here for things that are not used at least once a month. Everything else should either be stored in another place in your house, or be given away. Be ruthless. If you want to have an efficient, working kitchen, there is no room for clutter.

When assessing your kitchen's storage potential, examine every nook and cranny – from space between units and tiny alcoves or recesses to the backs of cupboard doors and the tops of kitchen cabinets. Then work out what food items and pieces of equipment you use most frequently. These should be stored as close to the area in which they are used as possible, as that way they are more likely to be put back in the correct place and will be close at hand when you need them.

Hidden Potential

The storage possibilities for the backs of kitchen unit doors are frequently overlooked. They can often be fitted with narrow shelves for small jars, spices, flavourings and condiments. The shelves should be in wood, wire or plastic with a small protective lip to prevent the items from slipping off when you open the door.

Larger doors, such as those opening on to walk-in pantries can also be fitted with shelves, baskets or bins suitable for more cumbersome items.

On Display

- Unused corners can be fitted with a tier of narrow shelves
- Pipes running down a wall can have shelves built around them
- The often unused space surrounding the door can be shelved and used for cookery books, household files, jars and decorative pieces of china
- And don't forget that all shelves can have cup hooks screwed into their edges to hold cups, jugs, sieves, egg whisks and so on
- If the room is high enough, iron ceiling racks are a splendid way to hang up bunches of herbs and dried flowers

ABOVE Slim storage shelves with sliding doors have been squeezed into a recess beside a wall-mounted double oven.

OPPOSITE ABOVE Squaring off odd-shaped corners with built-in cupboards is a good way of using the space.

OPPOSITE BELOW Shelves have been fitted under this splendid old sideboard to take glass and china.

It's a Great Idea...

- Use plastic, wood or wicker drawer tidies to keep small kitchen equipment in order. You can put these on open shelves and in cupboards, as well as in drawers
- Butchers' block tables mounted on castors and with drawer and shelf space underneath give you mobile storage as well as extra working space
- In a long, narrow kitchen, fix a chrome or dowelling rail all the way along the work surface, standing out about 2.5cm (1in) from the front edge. This can be used to keep tea towels and kitchen equipment such as ladles and spatulas handy as you work away
- There is often space left between units and appliances which can be used to stack trays or fitted with square compartments in which to store bottles of wine

SIMPLE LIGHTING IDEAS

It is important that the lighting in your kitchen combines good general lighting, task lighting above work areas and possibly accent lighting to pick up interesting objects or displays.

Lighting can make a great contribution to enhancing the feel of a room – whether it be a high-tech galley kitchen, a cosy family room or a combination dining and cooking area. And there is no other area in the home where it is more important that the lighting is good – when you are handling heavy objects, hot liquids and sharp knives, it is vital that you can see what you are doing in order to avoid accidents.

BELOW LEFT A lighting track set just above the countertop holds angled spotlights, providing a very flexible lighting option for modern, dual-purpose kitchens.

BELOW RIGHT A pair of wall-hung lamps with concertina arms has been taken out of the office and into the kitchen to flood the countertop with excellent adjustable light for food preparation, cooking and washing-up.

OPPOSITE RIGHT A deep wooden baffle neatly conceals the strip light fixed behind the recessed green area above these worktops. Lighting is gentle on the eyes.

Bright Lights

To supplement good central lighting, most kitchens need to have a variety of localized lighting over specific areas.

- ► Downlighters, spotlights or hanging industrial bulbs need to be carefully sited over worktops so that you are never working in your own shadow. Also ensure that you are not going to bang your head against them as you work
- ► Spotlights mounted on tracks so that you can alter their position are very flexible, particularly if individual lamps have their own on/off switches
- ► A successful alternative to overhead lighting is tubular lights fitted underneath wall-mounted cupboards with their glare diffused by battens
- ► Or you could always use simple clamp-on spotlights, but make sure that you are not overloading the circuit and that the flex is not trailing in a rather hazardous way
- ► Pivoting table lamps positioned under worktops can be used to direct light wherever it is needed
- ► Wall lights mounted on extendable 'arms' are particularly good positioned above the sink or work surface

Kitchen Diners

If the kitchen and dining areas are combined, the key to a successful lighting scheme is to relate flexibility to efficiency. If the dining table is used for homework and general household tasks as well as for intimate dinners, fix the main overhead lighting to a dimmer switch so you can change the lighting mood from functional to romantic.

An adjustable pendant light which can be raised or lowered is also a good lighting solution, providing general lighting when up and a focused light when down.

It's a Great Idea...

Maximizing the amount of natural light that your kitchen receives will make it a much more pleasant place in which to work.

- ► Choose a pale colour scheme which will reflect whatever natural light there is available. If you do prefer to have dark coloured walls, then at least paint the ceiling white or cream and use a pale floor covering
- ► If you have doors leading to the garden, glazing them will increase the room's natural light
- ► Likewise, replacing wooden panels on internal doors with glass will increase the natural light in the kitchen
- ► If your kitchen is located in a single-storied section of the house, investigate the possibilities of adding a skylight to the room
- ► Exploit the amount of light coming into the room to its fullest by hanging a mirror opposite existing windows

Instant Solution: PERSONAL COLLECTIONS

A wonderfully individual collection adds a bright personal touch to this very welcoming kitchen. LEFT

Instant Solution: ON THE RAILS

A kitchen rail is easy to install and can be used to hang saucepans and kitchen implements. BELOW

Instant Solution: HIGH TECH

Pipes and ducts have been highlighted in this high-tech kitchen – much cheaper and more imaginative than having them boxed in. Do remember, however, that some pipes may get hot and will need special paint. Most pipes and ducts will need to be primed before final painting with your chosen colour. LEFT

Instant Solution: PAPER LACE

White lacy paper doilies edging the shelves of this meticulously arranged glass cupboard are an unexpected but successful – and practical – extra touch. Cheap and easy to replace when they tear or start to look grubby, the doilies will help to prevent the glasses chipping. OPPOSITE

BATHROOM COSMETICS

A dull bathroom or gloomy cloakroom can be transformed with a good dash of imagination and enthusiasm

BATHROOMS ON A BUDGET

There are two schools of thought on ideal bathroom design. One puts functionalism first; the other advocates making the bathroom into a comfortable haven.

Putting the emphasis on function presupposes a fairly large budget for tiling all the surfaces; an efficient bath, shower and washbasin; good ventilation and heating; generous storage and good lighting.

The second approach – that bathrooms are for relaxing and soaking in, for reviving the mind as much as cleansing the body and, therefore, should be comfortable, decorative and personal – is not necessarily good for a family bathroom where short occupancy is appreciated. But it does lend itself to cosmetic treatments and the small budget. Whereas you need to aim for efficiency in a bathroom shared by several people, a small bathroom for no more than two can get away with a more glamorous treatment.

Bathrooms are traditionally one of the most daunting rooms to remodel because of the expense of plumbing and of new materials – and because this kind of work almost always imposes some disruption on your daily routine. But it is possible to minimize the costs and confusion by careful planning and by exploiting the full range of fabrics and materials available to the home decorator.

Beauty in Efficiency

Most modern bathrooms are quite small so it is easier to achieve an air of luxury for a comparatively small sum using expensive tiles, flooring and fabrics in small quantities. If you cannot afford such sumptuous treatments, there are still plenty of ways to revitalize the space with a little imagination and ingenuity.

- If you are stuck with a large expanse of tiles in an unappealing colour, clean them thoroughly before applying a coat of primer and then painting them with eggshell yacht paint followed by a coat of gloss paint for a lustre finish, or with epoxy paint
- A dull room can look more luxurious painted a rich, dark colour, then hung with prints, photographs and family mementoes
- Old wallpaper can be made to look a little more mellow and deliberately aged by adding a coat of polyurethane
- Or you could hang new wallpaper or even fabric, so long as you fix a perspex shield running around the top of the bath to the height of about 60cm (2ft). Fabric can also be coated with polyurethane to make it more durable
- Simple curtain treatments in filmy fabrics add a soft touch to even the most functional of bathrooms
- For a more streamlined effect, opt for a roller blind which you can either leave plain or decorate to co-ordinate with the rest of the room
- Old flooring could be replaced, either with tiles or vinyl floor covering, and can be softened by the addition of pretty mats or rugs
- Intersperse mirror tiles with ordinary tiles for a sparkling, glamorous effect
- Broken bits of glass can be used to make an unusual mosaic

RIGHT Soft blue tongued-and-grooved boarding makes this room look as pretty as it is functional.

OPPOSITE ABOVE Warm cream tiles are dressed up with a high black border and a black-and-white floor.

OPPOSITE BELOW A comfortable, turn-of-the-century look is achieved with cloudy blue faux *paper and stained mahogany.*

It's a Great Idea...

Unsightly plumbing can ruin the appearance of an otherwise pleasant bathroom. Try some of these easy solutions:

- ► Build a cupboard around ugly pipes and gain the added bonus of extra storage
- ► Construct shelves to cut across pipes and fill them with eye-catching bathroom bric-a-brac
- ► Make a 'skirt' for the washbasin with pretty fabric
- ► Paint pipes in bright colours to make them into a feature
- ► Let potted climbing plants grow all over them

BATHROOM FIXTURES

Handsome-looking fixtures are important features of every bathroom, but need not be bought straight from the showroom.

Damaged appliances can be repaired. As with kitchen sinks, baths, washbasins and lavatories can usually be professionally cleaned and resurfaced. If appliances seem beyond any hope of redemption, look around for second-hand models. Many builders and contractors have very good appliances in their yards which they have replaced with new suites. You could also haunt junk yards and demolition merchants where you might be lucky enough to find one of the much-prized old baths with claw feet or an old, decorated sink. If you decide to purchase a new suite, remember that white bathroom fixtures are much cheaper than coloured varieties.

New Lives for Old Baths

Consult your local telephone directory for the number of firms who carry out resurfacing on old baths, basins and lavatories. Or resurface baths and basins yourself with epoxy paint. You should have plenty of time and patience, however, if you are going to attempt to do this yourself.

- First, carefully prime the surface and then apply the epoxy either with a roller or spray can, following the manufacturer's instructions: make sure that you allow the recommended drying time for the appliance
- Decorate either the side of your bath or the bath panel in a complementary way to the walls

- For a sophisticated look, box in the bath and basin with inexpensive wood decorated with bolection moulding. This can then be given a mahogany stain, a coat of paint or covered in wallpaper – depending on the decoration in the rest of the room – then coated with polyurethane to make it water resistant
- Always leave at least one removable panel so that there is proper access to the plumbing
- If you are going to box in the bath, then consider building it out a little, to provide a good, deep shelf to hold bottles, jars, sponges and other bathtime paraphernalia.
- Stick shells to the wall in simple stylish patterns

Improved Relations

If you are going to fit new units and have the space, consider installing double basins. The extra expense can be easily justified by the much improved family harmony each morning!

LEFT Marbled walls, mirrors and chrome fixtures are set off by deep red accessories.

BELOW Stencil a border to add interest in your bathroom.

OPPOSITE Art Nouveau tiles and old furniture create a decidedly elegant bathroom.

SQUEEZING IN A SHOWER

Whether the squeezing involved in fitting a separate shower is financial or spatial, the effort is certainly worth it. Quite apart from the savings made in water and energy, showers are quick and easy to use, especially if more than one person is using the bathroom each morning.

You only need about 1 sq m (1 sq yd) of floor space to install a shower. One can be squeezed into the most unlikely corners, providing that adequate water supply and drainage are close at hand, and the water cistern is at least 1m (1yd) higher than the shower head to provide enough pressure for it to work efficiently. If this is not the case, a booster pump can sometimes be installed or the height of the cold water tank can be raised.

The cold water supply should, ideally, flow directly from the cold water tank and the hot water should be connected as close as possible to the hot-water tank to reduce fluctuations in temperature or pressure. An alternative model has a water heater adjacent to the shower head taking water directly from the mains and so does not require a tank.

Shower Solutions

- The simplest way to install a shower is over the bath. Apart from having it plumbed in, the only expense is the cost of a shower curtain or screen, which can be bought in a variety of colours and designs, from transparent to brightly coloured and textured.
- When installing a self-contained shower, consider very carefully before deciding where it should go. If you simply squeeze it into the most obvious space, you may end up with an awkward arrangement of space.
- As you will probably be employing a plumber anyway, consider whether it would be worth rearranging the layout of the bathroom completely.
- If the room is large enough, consider placing the bath in the middle as this will give you plenty of space around the walls for other fixtures.
- For a medium-sized bathroom, a bath centred on one wall instead of huddled at one end gives you all sorts of options – as well as having space for a shower cubicle at one end, the other space could be used for shelves, a basin and mirror, a lavatory or bidet, or even for an easy chair.
- Even in a tiny bathroom, there is often enough space to install a corner shower.

Quick Spray

Apart from the bathroom, there are plenty of other areas where you could squeeze in a shower, depending on your water supply. Here are some of the most popular spaces:

- In the corner of a bedroom
- On the landing
- Underneath the stairs
- Off the kitchen
- In a disused pantry
- In the basement

LEFT This sparkling white-tiled room is fitted with a sleek glass-doored shower across a corner. An awkward space has been put to good use with an effective solution.

OPPOSITE Glass bricks allow the installation of a shower in front of a window.

IT'S ALL IN THE DETAILS

Carefully chosen details make all of the difference between your bathroom being a cold, inhospitable place or becoming a favourite retreat in which to unwind.

After you have completed any remodelling or resurfacing work in the bathroom, it is time to consider how you are going to make this essentially functional space reflect your personality. There are many quick options open to you, from replacing taps (faucets) to hanging prints and photographs, using large terracotta pots instead of laundry baskets, and adding small display units or shelves for favourite collections of attractive objects.

Even if you are reluctant to carry out any remodelling, either because you do not own the house or because you are only going to be there for a short time, many of the instant style ideas that are outlined here can be achieved in an afternoon, so there really is no longer any excuse at all to live with a less than welcoming bathroom.

Stylish Extras

- New chrome, brass or primary-coloured plastic taps will add a polished feel to the bathroom
- Fine old taps can be re-chromed or re-brassed to add sparkle
- Shower heads are easily replaced with more efficient models, so long as the water pressure is good
- New lavatory seats are available in a wide range of colours or add instant distinction with a smart old-fashioned wooden seat
- You can buy other bathroom accessories such as shelves, cabinets, tooth-mug holders and so on to match any look
- Add the luxury of a heated towel rail, which is easy to install. They can be substituted for a regular radiator and are much more stylish
- A convenient addition is a wall-mounted hairdryer similar to those installed in hotel bathrooms (this is legal only in some countries)

Soft Touches

- A high, deep shelf lined with pretty baskets adds storage and creates visual interest
- Shower curtains can be stencilled to co-ordinate with the rest of the room or make your own using fabric and a nylon under-curtain
- If your bathroom is large enough, add an easy chair and a small table or bookshelf to create a special retreat
- The addition of glossy, healthy plants gives an instant facelift to any bathroom
- A set of lovely, fluffy towels adds a luxurious touch. You could give them a pretty border or appliquéd motif using spare curtain fabric

ABOVE Plain white tiles can be enlivened with stencils which you can easily make yourself. Seal them for added protection.

LEFT In a small bathroom, fix a shelf above the bath for extra storage. It will also provide room for displaying plants, attractive containers and other bathroom paraphernalia.

OPPOSITE Accessories in stainless steel or chrome are all-time favourites, look extremely smart and are relatively cheap.

INSTANT CHEER

Sometimes all that's ever needed is a flash of inspiration and a creative rearrangement of what you've already got

WALL DISPLAYS

Adding the important details that give a room its particular character is the most rewarding part of decorating. One of the most striking ways of doing this is by creating wall displays that reflect your own interests, your decorative tastes and ultimately tie the whole room together.

Almost anything can be used to brighten up your walls. Old quilts, beautiful pieces of fabric, old oriental or ethnic robes and needlework rugs all make wonderful wall displays. Heavier pieces can be hung from brass curtain rails; lighter or more precious fabrics can be framed behind glass.

Posters and paintings can be hung by subject or colour or used over an entire wall like wallpaper. Other collections, such as hats, old samplers, walking sticks and antique kitchenware can be hung in effective groups. And do not forget about unframed black-and-white prints, stuck directly on to the wall.

Pictures Posted

- A rather miscellaneous collection of prints, watercolours, oils, posters and even postcards looks better if at least some of the images are given a certain unity. Try matting them with the same distinctive coloured card, edged with a thin strip of shiny brass, chrome or polished wood
- Do not hang pictures too high or too far apart, or so low over sofas or armchairs placed against walls that people or furniture will knock against them. Hang them at eye level as much as possible, taking either standing or sitting levels into account
- Vertical arrangements of pictures, particularly those hung from long ribbons with bows and tails, will help make a room look taller, whereas a horizontal arrangement will make the room seem much wider
- Since small pictures are best hung in groups, you should decide on the overall shape of the arrangement beforehand and measure out distances carefully on the wall with a light pencil, or with chalk on fabric walls, both of which can be easily erased. Laying out your proposed arrangement on the floor is a great help
- Always think in terms of balance: a large painting balanced with a block of smaller paintings, drawings or prints of much the same size

ABOVE This collection of Egyptiana is contained within strikingly edged shelves topped with the head of Tutankhamen. A hieroglyphic frieze adds to the overall decorative effect.

RIGHT Quilts, rugs or blankets, of all shapes, sizes and patterns, can be used to add warmth to a room. They can also be used to cover up a less-than-perfect surface.

- Hang a large painting or large block of smaller pictures over a large piece of furniture such as a sofa
- Do not hang anything too heavy over a smallish piece

Instant Solution:
UTILIZE STAIRCASES

This staircase holds everything from seashells to rosaries, icons to folk art, all displayed to great effect against dark terracotta walls and black banisters. LEFT

Instant Solution:
KEEP IT POSTED

A simple letter-rack can be made from board, ribbon and drawing pins. Here, boards have been hinged together to make a screen. BELOW

Instant Solution:
FRAMED

Black-and-white striped paper makes a strikingly effective background for a carefully arranged collection of old baskets set in a black-and-white edged panel. It contrasts pleasingly with a set of plates on a black lacquer stand. OPPOSITE ABOVE

Instant Solution:
SHOW IT OFF!

Don't hide collections in drawers and cupboards – put them out on display. Here, an impressive collection of treen is full of character, but will need to be polished regularly to keep it shiny. OPPOSITE BELOW

SURFACE TREATMENT

As with most things, there are two opposing views about the display of possessions: the first is to give prominence to one or two particularly beautiful, rare or interesting pieces; the second is to display curious or personally important items with a studied randomness.

In the first case, the few possessions must be particularly distinctive, or at the very least made to appear so, or the effect will be sadly bare. The more cluttered displays need to be organized to best advantage, otherwise they will simply look untidy. For inspiration, study how the great still-life artists built up a composition using juxtaposition, colour and texture.

Streamline

- ► You can give objects the appearance of importance by placing them on glass or perspex shelves or plinths and lighting them from above or below
- ► If you want to display something on a side table, light it with a downlight placed immediately above. Given this treatment, even a bare, interestingly shaped branch in a jar, a luscious green plant or a vase of flowers will look wonderfully precious

Charming Clutter

- ► Collections of small objects should always be grouped together for maximum impact, rather than scattered around a room or house
- ► This applies particularly to the more homely collected objects such as shells, polished beach stones, pebbles, old spools, marbles and so on, which could effectively be displayed in glass jars
- ► Other fascinating collections, such as jelly moulds, old tinder boxes or card cases, toast racks, dice boxes, old bottles, or toys look good grouped *en masse* on side tables, ledges and sills

ABOVE RIGHT *Simple collections can make all the difference to a scheme.*

RIGHT *Store pebbles and shells in glass jars.*

OPPOSITE *This old wooden cupboard tones nicely with the boxes, bowls and sculpture.*

Instant Solution: NEW AND OLD

When storage is at a premium, as it frequently is in the kitchen, make full use of the walls for hanging kitchen accessories. Here, shiny copper saucepans look delightful suspended from a simple wooden bar above the kitchen sink. These saucepans are used and cleaned regularly and so always look attractive, but remember that dust and grease will collect quickly otherwise. Although this kitchen is of a modern design, all the decoration is old-fashioned, proving that new and old can work very effectively together. All the items on display are practical as well as decorative – the wooden salt box can be used to hide away scouring pads and brushes, the coffee mills can still grind coffee, and the ornate silver kettle is a viable and attractive way to keep the tea warm. Kitchen implements are always ready-to-hand in a rustic wooden container, while the floral storage jars, in contrast, are unashamedly pretty. ABOVE

Instant Solution: FISH-BOWL FUN

The accoutrements of a hobby can sometimes be turned to decorative advantage. Here, skeins of wool and coloured pencils are sorted by shade and placed in goldfish bowls where they are stored practically as well as being decoratively pleasing. The 'eyeball' lamps provide good task lighting and also accent lighting, highlighting the colours and textures of the wools. Kitchen storage jars are also very useful for this kind of display as their lids will keep the contents dust-free. Glass storage jars look particularly good on window sills where they provide privacy without restricting the penetration of light into the room. There are many different uses for this type of container: sand and shells would look good in a bathroom; cosmetics and jewellery could be kept tidy in a bedroom. Clear plastic storage containers are invaluable in children's rooms where they keep small toys off the floor while making a colourful display on the shelves. RIGHT

Instant Solution: KITCHEN EQUIPMENT

If storage space is in short supply, why not display your favourite pieces of kitchen equipment? Here, oriental cooking accessories, stool and hamper are set up in an unused corner on the floor with a whole batterie de cuisine *to form an unusual still life which is as useful as it is interesting. The grey roller blind is the perfect backdrop and complements the black wooden floor boards.* ABOVE

Instant Solution: COLLECTION DISPLAYS

A fine walnut chest of drawers is the perfect foil for a collection of bone necklaces, old perfume bottles and other Victorian dressing-table ephemera which are too interesting and eye-catching to be hidden away. The lamp, with its decorative, classical base, and mirror and drawer add height to the display. TOP

PLANTING IT OUT

It is astonishing the difference plants can make to a room. Whatever shade of green they are, whatever their shape or size, they instantly add a fresh, vital dimension.

Tall plants fill a bare corner, balance a large piece of furniture or dominant painting, juxtapose softly with sculpture and create subtle divisions within a room. Conversely, a table crammed with small, flowering pot plants adds colour, lushness and fragility where none existed before. And a bank of sculptural-looking plants such as cacti adds a textural dimension, as well as making a wonderful background for changing displays of seasonal flowers.

Seize the opportunity that plants present to the interior decorator and use them as one of your decorating tools, allowing them to reflect your taste and moods in a fresh, immediate way.

Green Fingers

Green, lush plants in pretty containers, carefully placed and shown off to their best advantage are of immeasurable benefit to any room, whatever its decorative state. Tired brown leaves and unhealthy stems, however, are to be avoided at all costs, so it is worth taking some care to investigate the types of plants that suit the conditions in your home before you even set foot in the garden shop. Good, sturdy plants are not inexpensive, and all of the money you spend could be wasted if they fail to thrive because they are simply in the wrong position or are not suitable for the environment.

Many modern homes are not conducive to healthy plant growth: air conditioning and central heating cause dehydration, and fan ventilation creates draughts which almost all plants dislike. Invest in an encyclopedia of houseplants and ask for advice when you purchase the plants – a good seller should be able to tell you what varieties would thrive best in your particular environment.

Plant Display

- Indoor trees placed on either side of an entrance, in front of or between windows, will make any room look grander while making ceilings seem to soar
- On a smaller scale, flowering plants add accents of colour, as do bowls of bulbs
- Baskets of plants on the floor beside seating, underneath glass- or perspex-topped tables, placed in front of fireplaces (in the summer), or in the centre of a table add a feeling of welcoming largesse
- Cache pots of plants on window sills, baskets of trailing plants hung in front of a window, small plants interspersed with glass objects on glass shelves across a window, will obviate the need for any fabric window treatment while adding their own, changing, decorative interest
- In a room of no great architectural interest, heaping plants on top of a wooden platform or some library steps creates an attractive, leafy balustrade which will make the space seem infinitely more appealing
- If you are going to group plants together, the same varieties generally look more natural together than a mixture (a clump of different sizes of the same species show variations on a theme)

Sweet Smell of Success

Do not forget sweet-smelling plants, particularly in winter. The delicious scents of narcissi or paper whites, hyacinths, frangipani and indoor jasmine are intoxicating and can often do more to make a room seem enticing than the most lavish decorative treatments.

LEFT Be dramatic! Plants are wonderful uplifters, providing colour and aroma in any interior. Branches with spring shoots are cheap and cheerful. The classical urns and unusual table vase are decorative elements in their own right and play an important role in the overall feel of the room.

OPPOSITE Remember to choose plants that match your decorative scheme, and make sure that the containers fit in too.

Instant Solution:
BATHROOM GREENHOUSE

Some houseplants positively thrive in the warm humid conditions of the bathroom. A ceiling-high Ficus *and an old pot full of white flowers add pleasing freshness to an already elegant bathroom.* ABOVE

Instant Solution:
YEAR-ROUND GREENERY

A table covered in different varieties of cactus will provide year-round greenery indoors. Cacti require little care and attention but their needles can be dangerous so remember to keep them out of reach of children. RIGHT

Instant Solution:
FLOWER POTS

Old terracotta flower pots are infinitely preferable to new plastic ones. ABOVE

Instant Solution:
PLANTING PRIVACY

Plants and flowers always look attractive when set against a window. LEFT

Instant Solution:
NATURE TAMED

This tiny corner demonstrates how greenery can add a sense of luxury. FAR LEFT

INDEX

Q

R

S

T

U

V

W

X

Y

Z

ACKNOWLEDGEMENTS

AUTHOR'S ACKNOWLEDGEMENTS

The author would very much like to thank the following:
Jillian Haines for designing the book so handsomely, Shona Wood and Abigail Ahern for the excellent picture research, Debora Robertson and Mary Trewby for all their work on the text, Abigael Sullivan for typing the text so efficiently and willingly, Alison Cathie, Felicity Bryan and Ray Roberts for their continual support, and most particularly Polly Powell, my editor, who I'd like to think was my special preserve but, alas, isn't.

The publisher thanks the following photographers and organizations for their kind permission to reproduce the photographs in this book:
10–11 Fritz von der Schulenburg (Andrea de Montal); 12 Ken Kirkwood; 13 left Fritz von der Schulenburg (Barry Ferguson); 13 right Fritz von der Schulenburg (Jill de Brand); 14–15 Fritz von der Schulenburg (Barry Ferguson); 15 above Tim Street-Porter/Elizabeth Whiting & Associates; 15 below René Stoeltie; 16–17 Michael Dunne/Elizabeth Whiting & Associates; 18 above Neil Lorimer/Elizabeth Whiting & Associates; 18 below René Stoeltie; 19 Ken Kirkwood; 20 Belle Magazine/Rodney Weidland; 21 above Paul Ryan/JB Visual Press; 21 below Belle Magazine/Garry Sarre; 22 above Andreas von Einsiedel/Elizabeth Whiting & Associates; 22 below Andreas von Einsiedel/Elizabeth Whiting & Associates; 22–3 Paul Ryan/JB Visual Press; 24 above Paul Ryan/JB Visual Press; 24 below IPC Magazines/WPN; 25 Derry Moore; 26 Tim Street-Porter/Elizabeth Whiting & Associates; 26–7 Jean-Paul Bonhommet; 27 above Graham Henderson/Elizabeth Whiting & Associates; 27 below Gilles de Chabaneix; 28–9 Bent Rej; 30 above IPC Magazines/WPN; 30 below Spike Powell/Elizabeth Whiting & Associates; 31 Paul Ryan/JB Visual Press; 32 Fritz von der Schulenburg (Jill de Brand); 33 above Jean-Pierre Godeaut; 33 below left Richard Bryant/Arcaid; 33 below right Fritz von der Schulenburg (Janet Fitch); 34 Derry Moore; 35 Michael Dunne/Elizabeth Whiting & Associates; 36 above Andreas von Einsiedel/Elizabeth Whiting & Associates; 36 below Ronseal Wood Style/Applewood; 36–7 Spike Powell/Elizabeth Whiting & Associates; 37 above René Stoeltie; 37 below Richard Bryant/Arcaid; 38–9 Bent Rej; 40 above Dulux; 40 below Derry Moore; 40–1 Tim Street-Porter/Elizabeth Whiting & Associates; 42 left Fritz von der Schulenburg (Richard Mudditt); 42 right Jean-Paul Bonhommet; 43 Jean-Paul Bonhommet; 44 above IPC Magazines/WPN; 44 below left La Maison de Marie Claire (Korniloff); 44 below right Hans Zegeers/JB Visual Press; 45 Twyfords bathroom suite (Camron PR); 46 Brian Harrison/Elizabeth Whiting & Associates; 46–7 Andreas von Einsiedel/Elizabeth Whiting & Associates; 47 Michael Dunne/Elizabeth Whiting & Associates; 48–9 Paul Ryan/JB Visual Press; 50 Bill Stites/Conran Octopus (Mary Gilliatt); 51 above Tim Street-Porter/Elizabeth Whiting & Associates; 51 below Bent Rej; 52–3 Jean-Paul Bonhommet; 53 Fritz von der Schulenburg (Miguel Servera); 54 above Jean-Paul Bonhommet; 54 below Rodney Hyett/Elizabeth Whiting & Associates; 55 Neil Lorimer/Elizabeth Whiting & Associates; 56 Jean-Paul Bonhommet; 56–7 IPC Magazines/WPN; 58 Rodney Hyett/Elizabeth Whiting & Associates; 58–9 Ed Ironside/Elizabeth Whiting & Associates; 59 Paul Ryan/JB Visual Press; 60–1 IPC Magazines/WPN; 62 Houses & Interiors; 62–3 Paul Ryan/JB Visual Press; 64 above Camera Press; 64 below Paul Ryan/JB Visual Press; 65 René Stoeltie; 66 Derry Moore; 67 Michael Dunne/Elizabeth Whiting & Associates; 68 above Fritz von der Schulenburg (Piers von Westenholz); 68 below Neil Lorimer/Elizabeth Whiting & Associates; 69 Andreas von Einsiedel/Elizabeth Whiting & Associates; 70 Neil Lorimer/Elizabeth Whiting & Associates; 71 above John Hollingshead; 71 below Rodney Hyett/Elizabeth Whiting & Associates; 72 above Fritz von der Schulenburg (Miguel Servera); 72 below Rodney Hyett/Elizabeth Whiting & Associates; 72–3 Michael Dunne/Elizabeth Whiting & Associates; 73 above La Maison de Marie Claire (Chabaneix/Puech); 73 below Bent Rej; 74–5 Michael Dunne/Elizabeth Whiting & Associates; 76 above Camera Press; 76 below Jean-Pierre Godeaut; 77 Roland Beaufre/Agence Top (Marie Elaine Blankaert); 78–9 IPC Magazines/WPN; 79 above right Michael Dunne/Elizabeth Whiting & Associates; 79 below right Jeremy Cockayne; 80 Derry Moore; 81 above left Tim Street-Porter/Elizabeth Whiting & Associates; 81 above right Camera Press; 81 below Guy Bouchet; 82 Andreas von Einsiedel/Elizabeth Whiting & Associates; 83 left Jeremy Cockayne; 83 above right Andreas von Einsiedel/Elizabeth Whiting & Associates; 83 below right La Maison de Marie Claire (Hussenot/Belmont); 84 Michael Nicholson/Elizabeth Whiting & Associates; 84–5 IPC Magazines/WPN; 86 above Rodney Hyett/Elizabeth Whiting & Associates; 86 below Neil Lorimer/Elizabeth Whiting & Associates; 86–7 Fritz von der Schulenburg; 87 Antoine Rozès; 88–9 Vogue Living/Geoff Lung; 90 left Bent Rej; 90 right Roland Beaufre/Agence Top (Garelli); 91 above Tim Street-Porter/Elizabeth Whiting & Associates; 91 below Bent Rej; 92 above Fritz von der Schulenburg (Gerard Bach); 92 below left Fritz von der Schulenburg (Peter Farlow and Mimi O'Connell); 92 below right Pascal Chevalier/Agence Top; 94 above Jean-Paul Bonhommet; 94 below IPC Magazines/WPN; 95 Fritz von der Schulenburg (Christophe Gollut); 96 above Jean-Paul Bonhommet; 96 below Camera Press; 97 Di Lewis/Elizabeth Whiting & Associates; 98 Ianthe Ruthven; 98–9 Rodney Hyett/Elizabeth Whiting & Associates; 99 above Gilles de Chabaneix; 99 below Fritz von der Schulenburg; 100 above Stylograph/Brackrock; 100 below left IPC Magazines/WPN; 100 below right Michael Dunne/Elizabeth Whiting & Associates; 100–1 Peter Woloszynski/Elizabeth Whiting & Associates; 101 Richard Paul/C Svec; 102 Camera Press; 103 left Bent Rej; 103 right Fritz von der Schulenburg (Andrew Wadsworth); 104–5 Jean-Paul Bonhommet; 106–7 Fritz von der Schulenburg (Barry Ferguson); 107 right IPC Magazines/WPN; 108–9 Paul Barker; 110 above Belle Magazine/Rodney Weidland; 110 below Spike Powell/Elizabeth Whiting & Associates; 111 above Bent Rej; 111 below Graham Henderson/Elizabeth Whiting & Associates; 112 above La Maison de Marie Claire (Primois/R Moreux); 112 below IPC Magazines/WPN; 113 Jean-Paul Bonhommet; 114 Kari Haavisto/JB Visual Press; 115 above Spike Powell/Elizabeth Whiting & Associates; 115 below Neil Lorimer/Elizabeth Whiting & Associates; 116–7 Fritz von der Schulenburg (John Stefanidis); 118 Fritz von der Schulenburg (Janet Fitch); 118–9 Debbie Patterson; 119 IPC Magazines/WPN; 120 Rodney Hyett/Elizabeth Whiting & Associates; 120–1 Andreas von Einsiedel/Elizabeth Whiting & Associates; 121 Yves Duronsoy; 122 Bulthaup; 123 above La Maison de Marie Claire (Darblay/Neuilly); 123 below Neil Lorimer/Elizabeth Whiting & Associates; 124 IPC Magazines/WPN; 124–5 Jacques Dirand/Stylograph; 125 right Spike Powell/Elizabeth Whiting & Associates; 126 Tim Street-Porter/Elizabeth Whiting & Associates; 127 Neil Lorimer/Elizabeth Whiting & Associates; 128 left Yves Duronsoy; 128 right Andreas von Einsiedel/Elizabeth Whiting & Associates; 129 Rodney Hyett/Elizabeth Whiting & Associates; 130 Fritz von der Schulenburg (Andrea de Montal); 130–1 Simon Brown/Conran Octopus (selected, designed, built and assembled by Pedro Guedes of Berman and Guedes Architects); 131 Antoine Rozès; 132 Yves Duronsoy; 133 above left Spike Powell/Elizabeth Whiting & Associates; 133 below left Jean-Pierre Godeaut; 133 right Neil Lorimer/Elizabeth Whiting & Associates; 134–5 Camera Press; 136–7 Fritz von der Schulenburg (Piers von Westenholz); 137 above right Jean-Paul Bonhommet; 137 below right René Stoeltie; 138 Fritz von der Schulenburg (Andrew Wadsworth); 139 above Andreas von Einsiedel/Elizabeth Whiting & Associates; 139 below Fritz von der Schulenburg; 140–1 Rodney Hyett/Elizabeth Whiting & Associates; 142 Camera Press; 143 below Dulux; 144–5 Belle Magazine/Rodney Weidland; 146 Fritz von der Schulenburg (Janet Fitch); 146–7 Bent Rej; 148 above Derry Moore; 148 below IPC Magazines/WPN; 148–9 Fritz von der Schulenburg; 149 Jacques Dirand/Stylograph; 150 Jean-Paul Bonhommet; 151 above Neil Lorimer/Elizabeth Whiting & Associates; 151 below Jean-Paul Bonhommet; 152–3 Jean-Paul Bonhommet; 153 Paul Ryan/JB Visual Press; 153 below right Victor Watts/Elizabeth Whiting & Associates; 154 Linda Burgess/Conran Octopus; 154–5 Jean-Paul Bonhommet; 156 above Spike Powell/Elizabeth Whiting & Associates; 156 below Jean-Paul Bonhommet; 157 above Spike Powell/Elizabeth Whiting & Associates; 157 below left Debbie Patterson; 157 below right Fritz von der Schulenburg (Barry Ferguson).